THE ENTWINING

A Journey of Transformation

J.S. Schmidt

THIS BOOK IS DEDICATED TO:

My Angels
Who lovingly protect and guide me.
I ask them to accompany me
Everywhere I go
And I know I am
Never without them.
That gives me courage and comfort.

- J.S. Schmidt

CONTENTS

Part 1: Spiritual Transformation

1. One 1
2. Two Faces Have I 4
3. Song For All Lovers 7
4. Hooked On A Feeling 11
5. All That Heaven Will Allow 14
6. Power In The Blood 19
7. Open My Eyes That I May See 22
8. Strange 25

Part 2: Musical Messages

9. Sweet Music Man 32
10. Do You Believe In Magic 36
11. Once In A Red Moon 39
12. Fire And Rain 41
13. Peace, Peace/Silent Night 44

Part 3: Communications and Gifts

14. Walk Through This World With Me 48

15. Under His Wings..50

16. Rock Me On The Water.....................................52

17. All My Lovin..54

18. Gypsy Woman...57

19. Isle Of St. Helena...61

Part 4: Intuition and Illumination

20. Lady..68

21. I've Got You Under My Skin...........................71

22. I Saw The Light...75

23. Precious Angel/Shine Your Light...................81

24. Candle In The Wind...84

25. Faithfully..87

26. I Am Your Angel...89

Part 5: Recurring Thoughts and Feelings

27. Reach Out I'll Be There....................................94

28. Smoke Gets In Your Eyes................................98

29. Lay Down Beside Me.....................................101

30. Mama...103

Part 6: Visions

31. Visions of Johanna..................................108

32. Angel Eyes..112

33. Wind Beneath My Wings....................114

Part 7: Dream Messages

34. Dream Weaver....................................118

35. Wedding Bell Blues............................120

36. The House You Live In......................125

37. Does Anybody Really Know What Time It Is?...128

38. Deep In The Heart Of Texas.............131

Part 8: Spiritual Snapshots

39. Snapshot...136

    A. Diamond Girl

    B. Glory Days

    C. Traces Of Love

    D. Fly Away

    E. In The Garden

    F. The Messenger

    G. Where Have You Gone?

    H. Wildwood Flower

    I. Born In The USA

Part 9: Animal Spirits

40. Butterfly Kisses..................................146

41. Wings Of A Dove...............................148

42. Run For The Roses............................151

43. The Eagle And The Hawk.................154

44. Forever Autumn................................157

Part 10: Guidance

45. Where He Leads Me..........................162

46. The Living Years...............................164

47. What's Your Name?..........................166

48. A Living Prayer.................................168

Part 11: Revelations

49. Coat Of Many Colors........................172

50. Just As I Am......................................175

51. All I Need Is A Miracle......................177

Part 12: Reflections

52. Funny How Time Slips Away............182

53. I Walk The Line...187

54. I Surrender All..191

55. I Hope You Dance..194

56. Feels So Right..196

57. Crystal Blue Persuasion..................................199

Final Word..203

PREFACE

The experiences and events related in this book are all my own. They are as true to my recollections as I am able to make them. Nearly all of the spiritual and metaphysical experiences I've had were documented by me within minutes or a matter of hours after they occurred. They are presented in my perspective because they are, in fact, things I saw, heard or felt. The truth of these experiences remains the same, though in some instances my perspective continues to evolve as other related events occur. What the meaning of these events is can change, for example, if other information is revealed to me as time passes. The first thoughts I have when interpreting these things may not always be right, but that doesn't change what happened; only what it is meant to show me. It is a learning process and I assume it will always be so.

~J.S. Schmidt

INTRODUCTION

The concept I had for this book; was to encapsulate all of the spiritual experiences I've had up to this point. I continue to have them almost daily. This book is an effort to present them in a "big picture" kind of way. I often feel like people don't know what I mean when I tell them about these experiences and that they can have them too.

When I began to look closely at my past, I realized these experiences were always happening; I just wasn't seeing them because my focus was almost entirely on the world and what was happening in it. It wasn't until my focus shifted dramatically after Ethan passed, that I realized what had been going on all around me all of my physical life.

I want people to understand these things are gifts that are meant to help us and teach us how to live our lives in the most meaningful way. Some of these things I have written about previously and I include them here because they are part of the "big picture" I am trying to present. I always hesitate to include something I've already covered in another book, because I don't want to be writing the same book over and over again. I try to remember that each of these books could be the only book I've written that an individual reader may ever have access to. In addition, though they are written in a sequence, it is likely they won't be read that way. If it seems a book would be incomplete without including these repetitive chapters, I include them; the reader is at liberty to exercise their right to skip over them, but I hope they won't because as I said: They are part of the whole story.

I have come to believe that every experience we have teaches us something. The key is to reflect on them long enough to discover what the lesson was that we needed to learn. Many people believe these lessons come around as many times as necessary in order for us to learn and progress. Once the message is received and understood they cease to appear in our lives. I at first, struggled to understand what lessons I was supposed to learn from the death of my son, but there have been many and each has helped me move forward in my grief and my journey to my eternal destination.

PART ONE:
SPIRITUAL TRANSFORMATION

1
ONE

*L*ike most people, I grew up believing I was a human being, who had a soul; no one ever mentioned the word spirit in relation to me as a person. I thought my life as a human being and my spirit were two totally separate things. I believed there was a worldly life and a heavenly life, and again, they were two separate things. As I have experienced spiritual growth in the years since my son's life was taken, I now see these things are interwoven and that they have never been separate. We live our spiritual life and our human life simultaneously. Our human life is the world of "time" and when our allotted time is over, we leave this world. Our spiritual life began long before we came into the world of time and it never ends. Until recently, it never occurred to me that the world of time is encapsulated within eternity. It is our free will, or choices that determine how entwined these two vines of life become. In order to grow beautiful and strong, each vine depends on the other and each needs to be nurtured.

When we reach the end of our human life and transition back to being solely spiritual, our human experiences are still part of us and they are not and cannot be separated from us. Our spirit exists eternally and our humanity is embedded in it forever. If you have ever questioned whether or not your departed loved ones will recognize you in the next phase of your life (as spirit), this is why I believe without doubt they will. Every human/spirit whose life has intersected with yours in any way has left its mark on your spirit. The imprint of it remains on your spirit as well as theirs.

I also believe that heaven is much closer than many people believe. It is a dimension that exists at a much higher vibration; everything in the universe is vibrating, including you and me.

Think of the sound of a dog whistle; it is so high pitched that humans can't hear it, our ears can't pick up vibrations on that scale. We know the whistle is making a sound because dogs react to it. A dog can hear many levels of sound above that which humans are able to perceive.

Similarly, a human being can't see gravity, but we know it exists because we see the results of it. Scientists tell us that without gravity everything on the earth would float away into space. When we see pictures of astronauts on the space station, they are floating around because they are outside the earth's gravitational pull.

There are tens of thousands of accounts by near-death-experiencers who tell of having seen colors in heaven that can't be found on earth; again, our eyes are only capable of seeing a portion of the total light spectrum.

In many of the books I've read, the universe is described as being like an onion: having many layers. If you think of earth as being toward the center of the imaginary onion and heaven being towards the outer layers, it is easier to think of them as simply different dimensions of the same space. Heaven isn't "out there" or "up there" somewhere beyond the clouds. It is a different level of consciousness, but exists as surely as the earth we walk on. Our human form isn't programmed to perceive the dimension we call heaven, but as we grow more spiritually conscious, we are drawn closer to that realm. It isn't as though we've never been there; our memories of it are blocked at the point of birth and we must rediscover it. It is where we originated and where we are being called to return to. NDES are proof that humans can sometimes slip through the barrier between these two dimensions, even though they haven't really passed from life as a human being. Many of these people are declared to be deceased, but are subsequently resuscitated and may live for many years following their temporary journey to heaven. Thus, it has become reasonable to believe that spiritual beings can cross the same barrier as frequently as they choose to interact with spirits in human form. The accounts of these visitations go back centuries. There has been voluminous research into this phenomenon by scientists, theologians, leading universities etc.

My own encounters with spirit beings, has become nearly an everyday occurrence and I am quite comfortable with them. I have learned to watch for and anticipate them. The reason for writing this book is to incorporate each of these experiences into a single volume, so that it becomes obvious to anyone who reads them in their totality, that this is an ongoing thing and that each experience affirms and supports the others. They are an ongoing conversation with the heavenly dimension.

2

TWO FACES HAVE I

My life has changed in many ways; I live a double life now. One life that is obvious to those around me, in a public sense. The other is the one I prefer to live more and more as time passes; it is my spiritual life.

My spiritual life is not to be mistaken for the "religious" efforts I made prior to my son's passing. That was what I thought at the time was leading me down the right path, but I'm not sure, at this point, that I would ever have truly arrived if I had continued on it.

Like so many other people, I spent years and years worth of Sunday mornings, sitting in a pew, going through the motions and wondering when it would hit me; the real meaning of what I was doing and why I was doing it. Don't get me wrong, there's nothing wrong or bad about going to church, it serves a very distinct purpose. For me and many other people, it didn't do what I expected it would do. It's kind of like going to school and never doing any homework; some of it has to take place inside yourself or you're only going to get part of what you need to know. It's kind of like the difference in standing and admiring a rainbow or being curious and determined enough to find what's at the end of it.

Spirit isn't to be found inside a church building only, nor does it reside in every church. Church buildings are just that; buildings where a service takes place that may or may not touch you spiritually. Spirit lives in each of us, because God placed it there; your task is to awaken your spirit to Him. Spirit is the key to living a meaningful human life. Attending a church can prepare you, but you have to recognize the spirit within you and turn it back to the One who created it and will feed and nurture it. It will cost you nothing that is worth holding onto to do this. It won't even cost you the free will God gave you; you'll still have it but it won't seem nearly as important as discovering what God's will for your life is.

When Ethan's life was taken, I knew immediately that I was changed; I would never be the person I was before that awful moment in time. I wanted so badly to turn back the clock to the second before that moment when Ethan was so suddenly and shockingly gone, I can't even accurately describe the chasm of darkness and emptiness I saw before me when I heard he was gone. I believed in that moment that what I saw was what my life would be going forward, until I myself departed this world.

Within a couple of weeks after Ethan's passing, I was aware of the definitive split in my life. I was living two distinctly different lives. My life as it appeared to others, was bleak and painful. My spiritual life was beginning to wake as if from a long sleep and its vibration increased with each passing day.

I had already experienced several life-changing spiritual events. Two weeks prior to Ethan's passing, my mother, who had been deceased for 13 years, touched my arm and warned me of an impending tragedy. Ethan had spoken to me in the car on the way home from Mississippi; he had been deceased 3 days when that occurred. I had by this time looked into Jesus eyes at the cemetery on the day of Ethan's service. When you are having these experiences, your day- to- day existence holds little interest for you.

I began to notice when I left my house and I ran into people who had known me all of my life, that I felt like an imposter, as if I was deliberately misleading people. They thought they knew who they were talking to, but I knew that person no longer existed and that she wasn't coming back.

It wasn't that I was doing anything deliberately to mislead anyone; it was a direct result of Ethan's traumatic and shocking passing. The suddenness of the devastation it caused deep in my soul, precipitated a nearly instantaneous spiritual transformation. The outside world was nearly impossible for me to cope with; there was no peace for me there and I needed to find balance and peace desperately.

My inner world, the world of spirit was calm and quiet and I felt so accepted in it. In the world outside myself, I felt anxious and doubtful. I began to search for a reason to live; a way to find meaning in a new life, because my former life was over and I could make no sense of what happened to my son.

I found meaning in the smallest of things in my spiritual world; butterflies, snowflakes, the chirping of the birds. I found purpose in writing and sharing my experiences. Helping others in some way gave my life meaning. Writing is something I need to do; I don't know if I'll ever want to stop doing it. As time has passed I have been able to better balance my time and focus between these two interdependent places; they have become entwined; as they are meant to be.

3

SONG FOR ALL LOVERS

The word entwined, means interwoven. Something that is interwoven is typically more than one strand or thread, such as a cord etc. One strand alone is never as strong as when it is woven together with another.

One of the purposes of this book is to show how the interweaving of the strands of a human life and a spiritual life enhances both. Many people regard those two aspects of life as being separate; ideally, they aren't, nor do I believe they are intended to be. Many people reject any acknowledgement of the spiritual aspect of their life, it is still there, it exists, but only as an unwoven strand. It therefore can't strengthen and enhance or give meaning and clarity as it is intended to do.

People often confuse religiosity with spirituality, they are not the same. Religion is defined as a system of practices and beliefs (Oxford Languages) usually as relates to an organized group of like- minded people. Spirituality is a personal recognition or awareness of one's own God-given spirit, implanted in our human body before birth. It is one part of us that will transcend our human existence to return to the source of all life. As given by God, it does not have a religious affiliation; it is not Protestant, Catholic, Buddhist, etc. Those identifiers are human choices, not Divine designations.

Spiritual living is not to be confused with religious practice or with occult practices (as defined by society today). The word occult actually means: supernatural, mystical or magical beliefs, practices or phenomena. Jesus performed miracles and they are by definition, supernatural. He did not practice magic, but His teachings are mystical or metaphysical in nature. Mystical means to inspire a sense of spiritual mystery, awe and fascination. One of the definitions of metaphysics is: transcending physical matter or the laws of nature. At the wedding in Cana, Jesus turned water into wine, a supernatural and metaphysical act, because it defied the laws of nature. This act could also be classified as being an occult practice, but not in the negative sense that the word occult means in today's thinking.

Many people have a strong aversion to the concept of spirit or spiritual practices based on the worldly representations of spirit as evil. Hollywood in particular, has realized a wealth of riches by presenting the idea that the spirits of those who have transcended (left this world) are evil, creepy, destructive and dangerous.

Many religious groups believe it is forbidden to associate yourself in any way with the spirits of those who have passed. It isn't the same as coming to know the spirit that is implanted within you; a living spirit.

Actually, there are no dead spirits, because spirit is eternal and can't die. When your body dies, your spirit departs from it and returns to God. It does not become evil and wish to harm people.

Your indwelling spirit is really the second half of who you are. Many of us confuse our ego with our spirit. If the voice you hear inside is telling you to do something you know is wrong, unwise or harmful, that is your ego, not your spirit. Your ego essentially operates singularly from your mind or brain; your spirit lives in your heart and functions best when your heart and your mind work jointly. Its guidance is often drowned out by the louder and more insistent voice of your ego and its need to dominate your thoughts. The spirit living within you is guided by The Holy Spirit, God's spirit of Truth and Wisdom and cannot give you false or negative messages. It is implanted by God and God is love and can't create anything other than love.

Love creates the need for us to connect with other spirits (people) and in connecting we begin to entwine our spirit with theirs. Think about the words from Ephesians 5:31, that are often used in wedding ceremonies: *"For this reason a man shall leave his father and mother and be joined to his wife, and the two shall become one flesh."* Many people today believe that scripture relates to the physical act of consummating a marriage union. I believe it instead means their lives (spirits) are to become so entwined that they become more one person than two.

People often mistake physical attraction, lust or common purpose for true love. True love is only achieved over time; it is a process of amalgamation, a combining or uniting of two things that once joined, create a new thing not formerly in existence. True love has to grow, mature and deepen into becoming "one Flesh". The entwining of hearts and bodies isn't enough to create true love; it must involve the entwining of hearts and spirits which over time, with constant nurturing and nourishment create true love's bond.

To a lesser degree, an entwining occurs when any two spirits connect and a bond of friendship begins and a relationship is formed that grows over time into a strong and meaningful union. When any of these bonds are broken by betrayal or death, we feel pain and loss because the relationship has become a part of us. The love of spirits who are separated by death cannot die; it is only transformed. When you come to know this, it lessens the pain of physical loss. We can still maintain our spiritual connection with those we love who have departed this life; it happens to millions of people. It happens to me every day; even after 6 years have passed.

I believe entwining begins automatically with a connecting or meeting of human beings, but in order to continue to grow, it requires a decision or intention to foster growth and a willingness to allow the entwining to occur. As human beings, we have the ability to prevent entwining from taking place if we choose to; it is a function of our free will.

Entwining with other spirits doesn't mean you are required to devote all of your energy or time to fostering deep friendships with everyone who passes through your life. It means that if you want to have deep meaningful relationships, this is the way it must happen. Entwining is a commitment to love.

4

HOOKED ON A FEELING

As human beings we are taught that we have five senses; we hear, we see, we touch, we taste, and we smell. We have also been taught to be suspicious of what we have named "intuition", as well as imagination. One of the definitions of intuition is:" direct perception of truth or fact". Another definition is: "The ability to acquire knowledge without using conscious reasoning". The general population might refer to intuition as: "having a hunch" or just a feeling about something. Intuition is sometimes referred to as the "sixth sense". Whatever you choose to call it, it is a tool that is available to us all and a sense that can be developed when you desire to do so. The only requirements are a degree of awareness that it exists and a growing sense of trust that it can be relied on.

I remember knowing I had this sense as a child, but I didn't trust it and was afraid to talk about it with other people. When my children were born my intuition about them proved to be very strong. In the past six years, it has become much stronger and something I am quite comfortable with placing my trust in. It has become a kind of guidance system that I pay very close attention to. It is a sense of knowing things without having or needing physical proof; it doesn't bother me that I can't prove what I sense to other people. It has become as normal for me to utilize this sense as it is to use the five senses I was taught to use as a small child. I can't help but wonder if children were taught about this sense, as well as the five senses we readily accept without question, how well developed it would become in the general population.

Intuition has become entwined with my earthly or human senses and often enhances one or more of them at any given time. One of the first things to learn about consciousness is that it has layers. Even when you are asleep, you are conscious, but not in the same way as when you are awake. Consciousness is described as "the fact of awareness by the mind, of itself and the world". It could also be described as:" the sense of being or existing". If you begin to study consciousness, you soon discover it is an incredibly deep subject and there is no end to the opinions and literature that has been written about it. My own writings and opinions about consciousness are completely unscientific; it is my own understanding and awareness that I speak of; in other words, I'm sharing how it works in my own life.

My intuition is very closely tied to my spirituality, which is not to say that it isn't or can't be independent of that part of me, but that it is greatly enhanced when the two things are interwoven. In my younger years, I thought of it as "having a strong feeling" about something. Now I recognize it as a "knowing" that you can't explain or justify, but it proves to be right many more times than not.

If intuition is calling me to take some action, I carefully consider it; I don't act on impulse. When I am convinced it is true guidance and is calling me to move in a positive direction, I follow its guidance. I don't want to be led down a rabbit hole and I don't want to do anything blindly. I don't want to cause harm to myself or anyone else. I don't want to mislead anyone. There are many false and negative influences in this world and I try to use caution and judgment as I walk my spiritual path. Many times, I ask for a sign to affirm that I understand the guidance I am receiving. When I receive an undeniable sign or more than one sign that confirms my thinking, I know I am following the right path.

    This guidance has become integrated into my life now and has replaced the doubt and uncertainty that often held me back. These days I have a healthy degree of skepticism, but I no longer allow fear to determine how I will live and grow spiritually.

5

ALL THAT HEAVEN WILL ALLOW

*I*n the wake of losing my son, I began to experience a series of truly amazing things and I needed to find meaning in these strange, yet wonderful occurrences. Once I started paying attention to them and recognized a pattern, I knew that they had actually begun much earlier than I at first believed. I was curious to know if other people were experiencing similar things; I wanted to know if they were spiritual, mystical, supernatural etc.; you could call them by any of those names. I wanted to know if the totality of my unexplained experiences had a name. Since I didn't know what to call it, I couldn't just google it or try to find it in a book at the library. Over time, I stumbled onto a couple of things that came close to explaining what was happening in my life.

The first, I found in a book; one of hundreds of books I read while searching for answers. It mentioned a "transformation of consciousness" that seemed to fit pretty well, but I had a feeling it was an incomplete explanation. That definition explained what happened, but not how or why it happened to me.

Recently, I discovered something that comes nearer to explaining my personal experience. I was watching a YouTube video about NDEs (near-death experiences) and someone used the term "empathetic NDE. My experience does not fit precisely into this category either, but I know it was a shared experience. However, typically an empathetic NDE occurs at the same time the death of a loved one is occurring, either in front of your eyes or hundreds of miles or more away from your physical location. My experience was delayed, but in nearly every other aspect similar to empathetic or shared NDEs. It was in the weeks and months following the murder of my son that I began to realize I myself had come close to death. I can't tell you, if indeed I was near to physical death or psychological death or some other iteration of death, but I know somehow, I came very close to not surviving what happened to my son. These experiences are famously difficult to explain in a way that makes sense to those who have not had them personally. I hope you will understand what I'm trying to relate in this chapter.

While no two NDEs or SNDEs are identical, there are many similarities and those two experiences share many similarities with what happened to me. The greatest similarities lie in the aftermath of such experiences. Since I have done a lot of research and you likely have not, I will attempt to give you a brief description of each of these events.

An NDE occurs when a person, for whatever reason, is clinically deceased; they have no blood pressure, no pulse, their heart is not beating and in many cases brain activity is absent. Many are in a death state for an extended period. This period has been substantially extended as medical equipment and life saving techniques have improved. People are successfully resuscitated today long after they would have been declared dead in the past. They show little to no brain damage, though the common expectation would indicate severe damage after a much shorter period of time, without vital functions in place. I will not go into the common explanation of many doctors and scientists as to how this happens; you can research that yourself; suffice it to say none of the standard explanations fit the majority of reported experiences.

Though most are initially reluctant to relate what they experience during this time of "clinical death", eventually the desire to share it overwhelms them and they begin to search for others who have had a similar experience. The hesitancy comes from the fear of not being believed or thought to be mentally unstable. These amazing experiences are believed to occur in approximately 20% of the population.

With some variations, the experience related often goes like this: They felt their spirit leave their body; usually through the top of their head. It rose high above the bed they were lying on. They are looking down at the body they recently occupied, that is still lying on the bed; most feel only a peculiar detachment from it. They are aware of what is taking place in the room below them; they hear everything being said and witness the lifesaving measures that the medical staff is performing on the body below them. They hear the sound of the monitors the body is attached to; most are sounding various alarm bells.

At some point they see what is most often described as a tunnel open up before them; they enter it with no fear or anxiety. They are rapidly propelled through the tunnel as they focus on a point of light that has appeared at the far end of it. The light is pleasant and makes them feel peaceful. The light grows larger as they travel toward it. They emerge from the tunnel and into the light; they perceive the light as energy that is embedded in every thing they see.

They are often greeted by a celestial being; some say an angel, others say it's Jesus, still others recognize deceased loved ones who've come to greet them. As they look around, they see topography that is very similar to earth; fields and meadows, forests and mountains, but all so much more brilliantly lighted than on earth. There is wildlife of every species and some unknown to us here. They see children playing and some see buildings which they are able to enter and observe the contents within them.

At some point, all describe a "life review", but they sense no judgement apart from their own. The review seems to focus on each interaction they had with other spirits while on earth; how did they treat others, were they kind and loving to those they interacted with. They feel the pain of any soul they have harmed and feel regret for such past actions.

When the review is completed, they feel forgiven and showered with love and peace. Then comes a time when they are made aware that it is not yet their time to be there and learn they must return to their body and live again. Most express reluctance to leave, but are gently returned to their abandoned body, that still lies where they left it. Most relate that re-entering their body is somewhat uncomfortable and it feels small and limiting after the freedom their spirit has enjoyed.

They are successfully resuscitated and after a period of recovery, they realize they are filled with a "knowing" that was not present with them before their NDE. Many come back with the knowledge that they have an unfulfilled mission to complete. Many are so changed by the experience that they make major shifts in their lives such as, a change of location or career etc. Many discover a new sense of purpose for their life. Only rarely, is an NDE reported to be frightening or unpleasant; most often they are positive life-changing occurrences.

Some of the resulting changes in attitude are truly amazing, things such as, the absence of a fear of dying. This often occurs in cases where the person lived all of their life with an intense fear of dying. Along with this is an increased sense of knowing that the afterlife exists and a longing to return there. Many people become much more openly affectionate and accepting of others. They return with a deep sense of gratitude to the Creator, for all they have received. They experience more joy, hope, and peace. They have a sudden clarity of thinking that was absent before their amazing experience. They know things they didn't know before and can't explain where the knowing originates. I expected to feel many things after losing my son, but gratitude was never one of them. My life is lived every day now, filled with gratitude and amazement at the love of God and the comfort I received in my darkest hours.

6

POWER IN THE BLOOD

I have often wondered if the world would be a different place, if we all understood the God-given power inside of us at an earlier age. It seems to take so long for us to find our personal power; our spiritual power. So many of us go through life feeling powerless; never realizing we can manifest our power from within. Spiritual power isn't the power that drives those infatuated with the world and all of its success driven chaos; it is the personal power that allows us to rise far above worldly trials and limitations.

Spiritual power is like high octane fuel; it gives us all the strength and stamina we will ever need to meet the daily challenges of life on planet Earth. In my belief system, this power comes to us through Jesus, but until we realize this power is lying dormant inside us, it can't be used in the way it was meant to be utilized. It is a miraculous gift and it is only our unawareness of it and the amazing heavenly energy contained within it, that prevents us from receiving its benefits.

As a child, I somehow came to know that contained within my human body, was a soul. I don't remember anyone saying that to me in a direct way and no one called it that. I think it was just something I heard about inadvertently, in Sunday School and worship services. I had a lot of questions early on in life, about my soul; where was it exactly, was it like my other internal organs, who put it there inside me? I didn't think of it as a soul, exactly, I thought of it more like a secret place that was hidden from everyone but me. It was my inside self; the real me that other people couldn't see. It was the part of myself that I held onto and was hesitant to share with anyone. I wasn't entirely sure at that time, that anyone else had an "inside" self, because no one ever mentioned it.

 I never asked those questions because I was shy and fearful of being judged for my ignorance of the answers. I don't know if it didn't occur to the adults around me, that a child would have these questions, and it was important for them to understand more than just the presence of a soul within them.

 My father often served as a lay minister and I spent much of my childhood years in settings where spiritual things were being discussed. My impression of those years now, and the instruction I received during that time, is one of vagueness. I was taught the usual things children learn at that age. I now realize there is a vast difference in Biblical study and spiritual knowledge. Knowing about Jonah in the whale, or Zacchaeus in the sycamore tree, etc. did little to answer my questions about my soul and what it meant to have one.

 I was taught about Jesus and the miracles he performed, but not in a way that separated them, in my mind, from modern day magicians. Miracles are not magic; they are not illusions or sleight of hand tricks. Miracles are a temporary suspension of the laws that govern the universe. The Oxford Dictionary describes a miracle as: a surprising and welcome event that is not explicable by natural or scientific laws and is therefore considered to be the work of a divine agency; Jesus or the saints etc.

 Most of my life I didn't expect to ever experience a "miracle".

I thought those things happened rarely and only to exceptional people; I thought of myself as pretty ordinary. I also believed that miracles occurred like lightning bolts and drew lots of attention; so many of my assumptions were wrong.

The spiritual power inside me lay mostly dormant until I uttered the words of a short prayer, early on the morning following the murder of my son. Those words were like the magic words Aladdin uttered to open the cave full of treasure. It was as if those words suddenly brought the sun, the moon, and the stars into perfect alignment and the door to heaven opened.

I have experienced many miracles; most of them I would consider to be small or minor miracles. I've come to realize that miracles don't come in sizes; there are no small, medium or large miracles. It is the impact they have that differentiates them. They are always a surprise and they are always heartwarming. Sometimes, they are an answer to a prayer and sometimes they come out of nowhere and are something so wonderful it wouldn't even occur to you to ask for it. I think they are all gifts to us and they reveal the true nature of God; His love, compassion, generosity and kindness.

"Which of you, if your son asks for bread, will give him a stone? Or if he asks for a fish, will give him a snake? If you then, though you are evil, know how to give good gifts to your children, how much more will your Father in heaven give good gifts to those who ask Him!"

Matthew 7:9-11

7

OPEN MY EYES THAT I MAY SEE

My spiritual eyes were opened through the tragedy of losing my son; it happened inadvertently. What I mean is: I didn't deliberately do or say anything with the intention of making it happen. I believe it happened through my plea for help, in the early morning hours of the day after Ethan's life was taken.

I didn't ask for spiritual sight; it is a by-product of my asking for divine help. In total surrender, total emptiness, I asked God to help me survive a loss that I knew could possibly destroy me, if I was weak enough to let it. I knew I had no strength of my own; at that moment, I barely had enough strength to stand or walk.

Never have I had such feelings of utter hopelessness and helplessness. I am ashamed to say that prayer wasn't the first thing to enter my mind, when I learned what had happened to my son. I do remember asking the pastor who showed up at my house that day, to pray for me.

The next few hours were something of a blur; my two other sons and their families began to arrive at my house; friends seemed to show up out of nowhere to offer their help and condolences. I had to pack some things for the trip to

Mississippi. I had promised Ethan's wife Liz, we would come as quickly as we could.

It was only after I was settled in Jeff's car later that afternoon, that I was able to focus on my feelings. I spent at least 7 hours of the 11- hour trip to Cleveland in complete hysteria; I wasn't screaming or hitting things, I was weeping uncontrollably. I was cognizant that I wasn't the only person in the vehicle that was traumatized. My son, who was driving, had been up since 5:30am, when he got up for work and Tom had been up since 6:30am, when he went to work also; he was in a meeting when I called to tell him what had happened to Ethan. They were both calm on the drive to Mississippi, but clearly stunned; they rode nearly all of the 11 hours in silence.

When we were finally settled in a hotel room around 3:30am on the day after our son's life ended, I knew they needed to rest and so did I. I doubted I would actually sleep, but I laid down on the sofa bed in the room and began to wrestle with the enormous loss I had suffered. I realized it was more than I was capable of handling, so I uttered a short prayer. I knew God was there and that He heard my words; what I didn't know was how or when He would respond. After I prayed, I tried to go to sleep, but couldn't; what happened next is detailed in the chapter of this book, titled: The Isle of St. Helena.

When I prayed in that hotel room, it wasn't my intention to open a portal into heaven; I wasn't looking for an access point, but somehow that is what happened. Senses became activated that I never knew existed.

The senses that were activated then, remain active to this day; they are what makes it possible for me to live in this world without my son. I believe these gifts were given to me to assist me in creating a new life, so I could go on living. They brought me a sense of purpose; they brought me the realization that it was important for my own recovery and wellbeing that I share my experiences as openly, truthfully, and completely as I could. Writing has become so meaningful to me because I believe there is a reason for me to do it, that goes much farther than the comfort it brings to my own spirit.

8

STRANGE

To the average person, it may sound strange to hear someone talk about the world of spirit; I can understand that completely. We have been given many negative images with which to equate this topic. Most of these images are created by the entertainment industry and have nothing at all to do with the reality of the world I'm speaking of. The world of spirit is a real thing, it exists, it isn't really hidden, it just goes unnoticed most of the time. It isn't spooky or sinister, although it can be made to appear so. The world I speak of is free of negativity; the "evil" that Hollywood repeatedly portrays isn't a part of this world. That is something else entirely. My experiences have shown me that a negative force does exist, but I believe it is a result of man's actions and negative thinking.

In the previous books I've written, I told several stories of my personal experiences with spirit and I want to include those accounts here as well, in an effort to create a complete record of them. I hope, when viewed in their totality, you will conclude that the world of spirit is a real thing and something you can experience if you choose to.

If you are reading this and you don't know me personally, let me tell you a few things about myself. Those who really know me would likely tell you I'm a pretty normal, down to earth person. I'm very practical and think rationally and logically. I began to have spiritual experiences at a fairly young age, probably around 10 yrs. old. With the exception of a couple of these experiences, they have never been frightening; most of them were just somewhat puzzling and it sometimes took years for me to understand their significance. It was after Ethan's passing, that I really began to look at them closely. It was just prior to losing my son that I had one of the most amazing and surprising interactions with spirit.

My mother passed away January 16, 2002, from cancer. I thought about her every day of my life, until my son's life was taken and my focus shifted to overwhelming grief at the loss of my child.

Usually, when I thought of my mother, it was something she said or did that made me laugh. She had a big sense of humor; it was perhaps the biggest part of her. In stature she was a very small person; her personality was huge.

One morning in late August of 2015, I sat down in the back parlor of my large Victorian home (The TV room), to take a break from cleaning and enjoy a cup of coffee; it was around 11am. I briefly closed my eyes, but was fully awake when I felt someone touch me gently on my upper left arm. It startled me because I knew I was home alone and the doors were locked. Before I had time to think about it, I jumped out of the chair; the instant I was in motion I knew it was my mother who had touched me. At that time, she had been deceased for over 13 years. I had moved involuntarily; from that moment to this one, I wish I had been able to sit quietly and see what would have happened next.

The chair I was sitting in was a glider rocker with a footstool directly in front of it; I realized I had somehow propelled myself out of the chair and over the footstool, spun around in the air so I was facing the chair, and then my feet touched the floor. I have yet to figure out how all of that happened in one motion. I wasn't afraid because I knew it was my mother's spirit that had touched me; I was startled because nothing like that had ever happened before and up to that point, I wouldn't have believed it was possible.

    I didn't see my mother; I only felt the touch that was as real as if I touched you at this moment. I heard no audible voice, but I received a message that I knew came from her spirit. The message was: *"Something is coming, and you need to brace yourself!"* At that point in time, I assumed the message referred to my father who had been on hospice care for several months. I thought it must mean he would soon pass away. Most of 2015, I had lived with an undeniable sense of foreboding; I knew something bad was going to happen. I didn't know who it involved or when it would occur or what would take place; I only knew something was coming. Approximately 2 weeks later, Ethan's life was taken by a colleague at the university where he taught. I felt like my mother was so concerned about how I would react to losing Ethan, that she knew she had to prepare me in some way. It would seem obvious that she knew in advance what was going to happen.

    I used to dream about my mother after she passed; it wasn't the same dream each time, but it was very similar. I still think about her often, but not every day like I used to. The thought has often crossed my mind that I'm glad she wasn't here when Ethan's life was taken; my own grief was so overwhelming and I know I couldn't have borne seeing hers. I am thankful she saw this tragedy from another place and with a far different perspective. I know they are together. My father passed about 3 months after Ethan; we never told him what happened.

He was suffering from Alzheimer's and he would only have remembered for a short time, but I didn't want him to feel that pain even for a moment. Ethan was there with my mother to greet Dad on the other side of the veil and I'm sure he was shocked to see him there.

   In the chapters that follow, I will relate many of the experiences I've had that involve spirit; not the hooded or cloaked kind that you see in movies, or at Halloween, but interactions that come from another dimension that people commonly refer to as heaven. This is spirit that consistently fills what seems like empty space all around us. Spirit that coexists with us, but at a higher frequency than our own. Does it not make sense to you that as human beings continue to evolve, our own vibrational frequency moves ever closer to that of our place of origin; our home?

A Journey of Transformation

PART TWO: MUSICAL MESSAGES

9

SWEET MUSIC MAN

The first messages I received from Ethan following his passing, came through music; they were completely spontaneous. I had no idea communication with any deceased person was actually possible. The fact is that you don't communicate with a deceased human, but with the spirit that inhabited their living body. I knew about mediums and I didn't totally discount their ability to communicate in this way, but it never occurred to me that I could be capable of such contact.

It wasn't surprising to me at all that Ethan would use music to communicate; he was such a lover of all genres of music. My parents were both musicians and the most obvious legacy they gave to their family, is a love of music. I can't think of a single member of my family that doesn't love music; we either listen to it every day, sing it, play it or talk about it!

The first musical communication from Ethan came on the third day after his spirit departed. I was in the van that he and Liz owned, traveling down the highway, as we returned home from Mississippi for his service and burial. Hearing his voice that day was the second greatest shock of my life; second only to the news that he had been murdered.

As I became attuned to the musical messages, which evolved

over the next several months, I began to discern patterns in what I will call the" musical code" he uses to speak to me. Sometimes he would use a particular song to get my attention; for instance, "Brown-eyed Girl" by Van Morrison. I always told him that was my song, because it is one of the few songs written about a girl with brown eyes. Other times, he would use a series of songs played consecutively, to get my attention. I began to recognize certain songs that he used to identify individual people that he had something to say to or about. I could name a song he used to identify each member of our family in his messages. When Ethan and I converse through music, I turn Pandora to a station that plays most of the songs I heard the first day he spoke to me after his passing. As soon as I hear something in a song that gives me a clue about who or what he wants to talk about, I stop the music and listen. I write what I hear him say. When he stops speaking, I turn the music back on and wait for the next song.

This process is repeated with each song until I hear several songs in sequence and there is no discernable clue as to a message. This type of communication has occurred hundreds of times in the six years since his passing; I often hear his voice telepathically telling me: *"turn on some music, Mom."*

As time passed, I realized that I could initiate contact with him whenever I wanted to by writing him a letter and then waiting quietly to hear his response. I would write his response in the form of a letter addressed to me.

You might ask why he used musical messages if it were possible for him to speak to me in a more direct way. His explanation is that initially, I was so overcome with my grief and pain that I couldn't hear his voice; he used the music as kind of a last resort. He still often communicates in the musical code simply because he enjoys it and it creates an opportunity for us to listen to music together, just as we did in his physical life.

The biggest difference in these two ways of communicating is that when he uses the musical code, he is directing the conversation; when I make the connection by writing to him, I am directing the conversation. My informal research with spirit communication reveals there are numerous ways for contact to be made. Consider the various ways humans make contact with each other: we talk on the phone, text, email or participate in Facebook. In the low-tech world, which is mostly where I prefer to hang out, we write letters, send cards or flowers etc. Humans also send messages through music; many couples have a special song that relates their feelings for each other. Many people have a special anniversary song, other songs evoke memories of special times in our lives. It has often been said that "music is the universal language." Music can touch our hearts even when we don't understand the language the lyrics are written in.

I often hear songs in these communications with Ethan that I can't relate to an individual person, but they carry another kind of message, such as: "Pachelbel's Canon", Ethan and Liz's wedding song, is one he uses most often to tell me goodnight. I listen to music every night as I'm falling asleep and I hear that song almost every night; sometimes I hear multiple versions of it in about an hour. Ethan always tells me he loves me in his letter responses, but sometimes he says it with a song, one such song is: Everything I Own", by Bread. Another song he frequently uses to convey his love for me is, "Longer", by Dan Fogelberg. These are just a few examples; I could give you hundreds.

I hope this explanation gives you a better idea of what this kind of communication is like. At the back of each of my books is a list of song credits for each song used as a chapter title, or that is used as an example to make some point or other. They are all great songs and I'd love it if you were inclined to listen to the songs; just a suggestion; they speak for themselves.

10

DO YOU BELIEVE IN MAGIC?

There aren't many people who don't like music in one form or another, but some of us are more in tune with the magical quality it possesses. It can express so many different emotions and it can transport us to other times and places, it can evoke beautiful memories of special occasions or memories of loss. There is a certain note in Eric Clapton's rock anthem" Layla", that is so evocative that it almost speaks a human word. Albeit, not a happy word, but almost certainly a desperate word of longing. When I hear it, the mysterious word is right on the tip of my tongue, but I can't quite find it; music that can do that is pure genius. Music has the ability to heal wounded hearts, sympathize with hurt feelings, calm our anger and lift our mood. I can't even imagine how much darker and sadder the world would have been if God hadn't given us music.

My first introduction to classical music came in third grade, via our music teacher Mrs. Windsor. She began to spend a portion of every class playing classical selections while we were supposed to sit quietly and try to feel what emotion the music evoked in us; most of the kids found this a very boring exercise. I have to say there were times that I did too, but there were a couple of pieces I found myself fascinated with. The one I really liked was "Scheherazade" by Rimsky-Korsakov. It was inspired by the collection of stories known as "The Arabian Nights"; the composer often looked to fairytales for inspiration. The other, which I found interesting but did not particularly like was "Flight of the Bumblebee", which was also composed by Rimsky-Korsakov, as part of an opera called "The Tale of Tsar Sultan". It fascinated me because the music sounds just like the title; you can easily imagine a swarm of bumblebees in flight. I thought it must be a very thrilling thing to be able to make individual notes come together to illustrate exactly what you wanted them to.

Ethan developed a love for classical music at an early age; he was probably just into middle-school. As he was discovering classical music for himself, he wanted to share it with me and introduced me to some of the composers whose music he enjoyed. He gave me a box set of "The Four Seasons" by Antonio Vivaldi. It was something he liked to listen to when doing homework and later as he wrote books related to his field of study. We used that box set as the prelude to his Celebration of Life service.

As I grieved the loss of my son, I found myself listening to Vivaldi frequently as I went to sleep at night. The following year my son Jeff gave me a" Sonos" speaker as a Christmas gift. I didn't even know what it was, but he assured me I would like it, and I certainly did. I liked it so well that we now have them in the bedroom, kitchen, basement pool room and in my sewing room upstairs.

Another of Ethan's favorites was George Winston. Tom's brother Dan also liked George Winston; I think he probably introduced Ethan to that music, so I thought George Winston's arrangement of "Pachelbel's Canon" would be an appropriate selection for the pianist to play at Dan's Celebration of Life service. On April 9, 2020, about a month after Dan's passing, I wrote two chapters for the book I was writing at the time. In about two hours of writing those chapters, which were about Dan and Ethan, I heard Pachelbel's Canon at least 5 times. These things always reinforce my belief in the power of music to speak to us and in the belief that spirits live eternally, they are around us all the time, and they try many different ways to get our attention.

11

ONCE IN A RED MOON

In my book "Roses and Thorns", I related the story of the lunar eclipse that occurred on the night of what would have been Ethan's 40th birthday. I will retell it here, with a slight addition to the story that only occurred recently.

Ethan's 40th birthday was Sept. 27, 2015, exactly two weeks after his life was taken. Everyone who loses someone has to endure that first painful year of birthdays, anniversaries etc. without their loved one. I expected this special birthday to be a devastatingly painful experience; surprisingly, it wasn't. I guess the reality of his absence was just so new, that it hadn't really landed on me yet.

The "Blood Moon" lunar eclipse that occurred on the night of Sept. 27th, 2015, took on a special and very spiritual significance for me. It was the first time in my life I had ever experienced this type of eclipse and the fact that my son had so recently transitioned to a celestial dimension, made it highly emotional for me.

Moving forward to March 10, 2020; the night my husband watched his younger brother Dan transcend the boundaries of physical existence. Our family and about 600 friends, colleagues and students said goodbye to Dan C. Schmidt; son, brother, husband, father, uncle and amazing theater director on Saturday, March 14, 2020. As I sat beside Tom in the Celebration of Life service for my brother-in-law, I looked directly at the large portrait of him on the stage, several times. Each time he seemed to be looking right into my eyes and I heard him say *"Suz, don't cry!"*; it happened at least three times. Because I had the experience of Ethan speaking to me 3 days after his passing, I wasn't the least surprised that I would hear Dan speak to me during his service.

   A couple of days later, I was thinking about Dan and I wondered if he had arrived in the place where Ethan's spirit now resides? I asked Ethan to give me a sign if Dan was with him and then I waited. About 3 hrs. later, as Tom and I sat in our darkened TV room, listening to my Enya station, I heard a song I didn't recognize. I picked up my phone to see what was playing; to my surprise the name of the song was "Once In A Red Moon." There was the sign I had asked for. The only person I can connect with a red moon, is Ethan.

Ethan and Dan in younger years. They shared many common traits and common interests.

12

FIRE AND RAIN

We have just passed another Mother's Day; the sixth one since my child's life was taken. It is the hardest day of the year for me to get through. I tell myself every year, it's just another day, but saying it doesn't make it so. Each year as Mother's Day approaches, I think to myself: *"maybe it'll be okay this time."* Then about a week before, I begin to feel my emotions are building. This year was better than last year and it seems to be a little better each time. There were still some tears, just not as many. I sometimes wonder if I'll ever just let it pass with no pain.

For the majority of people, Mother's Day is a pleasant opportunity to celebrate and show their love for a mother figure in their life. I began to feel differently about Mother's Day when I lost my mother to cancer 19 years ago. For those of us who have a child missing from their life, it is a day when we remember someone who brought us joy and happiness; someone whose memory is often tinged with pain. I have thousands of happy memories of Ethan, but many of the most memorable are now tinged with sadness.

On Mother's Day, there will be no phone call or beautiful sentimental card or bouquet of flowers sent with his love. Every other day of the year, I am able to celebrate the incredible gift I received on Sept. 27, 1975, my son Ethan, but on that one day each year, I think of my loss.

In my acquaintance are many mothers of deceased children; I recognize my pain in their eyes and in their spirits. I have often wondered why I know so many people who have suffered this kind of loss? I can't say for sure, but I feel as if writing about my personal loss, might in some way help someone else; someone who wonders if they're going crazy with grief. Just letting them know they are not alone in these things seems to help. That is why I write and why I share my story as often as I can. I'm sure there are some who wonder why I can't just move on; the answer is that this is my way of channeling my grief into something that helps others and in doing so, it helps me. When someone tells me, they have been touched in a positive way by something they read in one of my books, I am given a gift of healing. Whenever grief is shared, the pain is eased and the burden becomes lighter.

In my first book, I included a chapter titled: The Village Lanterne; I am repeating some of that here because it includes a supernatural experience related to Mother's Day:

On April 27, 2016, approximately ten days before Mother's Day, I listened to Pandora, as I did nearly every day, hoping to receive a message from Ethan. Sometimes, the messages would start as soon as the music began to play and other times I would listen to song after song, that held no meaning for me. That day the first six songs that played were meaningful. The next was a song I very much like, but it held no meaning at that moment, so I began to think the message from Ethan had ended. Then, a beautiful, haunting melody began to play; I had never heard the song before and was unfamiliar with the group performing the song. As soon as the woman began to sing, I started to cry. The lyrics were so beautiful and meaningful; I knew it was a special message—a gift, if you will, from Ethan. When the song ended, I received this message from him: *"I know Mother's Day is coming and I know you'll be sad. I don't know what to do about that. Please, try to celebrate the gift we were both given, when I was born as your child. You're still my mom, and I still love you more than you could ever know. Remember that last hug. Remember the first moments we spent together and every precious moment in between. I love you!* (it was at this moment that I heard The Village Lanterne). *"You weren't supposed to cry, Mom. I knew you would love this music. It's your Mother's Day gift from me. I know you'll always think of me when you hear it. Time to close now, no more tears, ok? Love, Ethan"*

I bought the CD the song was on and I play it often when I'm driving; it still makes me very emotional and I feel even closer to Ethan when I hear it.

I am immensely grateful for the three children I was given and I celebrate each of their lives and how they have entwined with mine; I can easily do that on every other day of the year. I wrote the following prayer this year on Mother's Day and I would like to share it:

Heavenly Father,

I ask your blessing of comfort, strength, hope, courage and healing on all mothers who mourn their lost children. May they find peace and joy in Your great love and infinite compassion. May they recognize Your angels of love and protection, who walk beside them each day. May they look up from their grief to find themselves looking into the eyes of the Lord, who weeps with them and feels their loss so deeply. In You, Father, is the only comfort to be found.

In Jesus Holy Name,
Amen

13

PEACE, PEACE / SILENT NIGHT

One of my favorite Christmas memories, comes from the time my kids were going through high school. Ethan always loved to sing and was involved in vocal music classes and choir. Each year the choir closed the Christmas program with a beautiful presentation of the song I have chosen for the title of this chapter. The choir would finish their next to last selection and then exit the stage to an area at the back of the auditorium; a hallway. When they re-entered, they came back down the aisles carrying lighted candles and singing: Peace, Peace; there are several verses. At the appropriate moment, the pianist began to play Silent Night and the crowd sang along, as the choir brought the song to its conclusion. The words are a call to joy, love and peace. It was always such a beautiful, heartwarming experience that brought home to me and many others, the true meaning of Christmas.

Over the years, I forgot the name of the song, but the warm memories of the experience stayed with me. I tried to find the song, but that proved difficult because I didn't have the right name for it. My sister found it for me and sent it to me on her iPhone, with a video of a choir performing the song. Hearing it again, brought a vision of Ethan as a teenager, walking past me in the candlelit auditorium, as he came down the aisle. The memory is so precious, and it brought floods of tears, to see him as a young man; the way I often picture him in my mind now. I had no idea hearing the song again would evoke such a strong reaction; those were such good and happy years in our lives, when our family was all with us.

It took me a while to regain my composure, and that only occurred when I forcefully put the memory out of my mind. I struggled all evening to keep it from upsetting me and when I turned the light out to go to sleep, I was still struggling. I turned on Pandora, as I usually do while I'm falling asleep, and the first song that played was: "Pachelbel's Canon", the song Ethan uses to tell me goodnight. The second song was: "Once In A Red Moon", the song I identify with Ethan, because of the blood moon eclipse that occurred on his birthday, two weeks after he passed, and also with Tom's brother Dan, because I heard it for the first time the evening of his burial. Hearing those two songs back- to- back, let me know Dan and Ethan were there together to support me. I went to sleep smiling.

The Entwining

PART THREE: COMMUNICATIONS AND GIFTS

14

WALK THROUGH THIS WORLD WITH ME

The first time I heard Ethan speak to me, following his transition, was in the car when we were returning home for his service and burial. The second, was on the day of his service, as I stood in line to walk into the gymnasium where his service was set to begin. Before I took the first step into that cavernous room filled with people, Ethan whispered in my right ear: *"I'm right here, Mom. Just be calm and we'll get through this together."* He spoke to me again during the service, at a point when I was about to lose my composure, he said: *"It's okay, I'm right here."* Again, the voice seemed to come from behind my right shoulder. With Ethan's help, I was able to make it through the service without shedding a single tear. I was dreading such a huge public event, because I wasn't at all sure I could maintain my composure and I hate crying in front of other people. I wanted to honor my son, not make a spectacle of myself. Hearing Ethan speak to me at his service, convinces me that it is possible that all spirits attend their own funeral or memorial services. Now, when I attend those services, I am able to open myself up to feeling the presence of the one being mourned, instead of feeling the loss. I know they aren't really lost at all. I know they are so very close to us.

As time has passed, Ethan and I have fewer formal communications, because I realize he is always just a thought away. It feels as if he has been absorbed into my skin and I don't need to seek some form of communication to reach him. We still talk, but it's as easy as breathing. If I want to have an actual conversation with him, I can turn on some music and listen for his voice, or I can sit down and write him a letter and then wait to hear his reply. Once, when I was writing spiritual poetry, I realized he had taken over and written the last couple of verses. I believe everyone can have this kind of closeness with their loved ones in spirit, if they are truly open to it.

15

UNDER HIS WINGS

I keep trying to wrap this book up, but even as I'm in the editing phase, more and more experiences occur.
I recently had lunch with an old friend I had lost contact with for many years. We came together again after both of us lost a son. My son, Ethan passed in 2015 and Karen's son Jon, passed in 2016. During our recent lunch, Karen asked me if I ever heard from another of our classmates; her name was Stacy. We met on the first day of 7th grade and instantly became friends; we each had other friends, but we were "best friends" for over 30 years. As time passed, our lives went in separate directions and around 1995, we lost touch. She moved from the town she had lived in for many years and I had no phone number or address for her afterward. I answered Karen's inquiry about Stacy with regret; I had no information to share.

When I arrived at my sister's house later that day, I began to relate my conversation about Stacy to Jeanne. Out of curiosity, Jeanne tried to find Stacy on Facebook; I was shocked to learn that she had passed three months prior to our search. It really disturbed me that she had been gone for that length of time and I knew nothing about it. Had I known she was ill, I certainly would have made every effort to see her.

Her death had a much bigger impact on me than I would have thought, even though we hadn't been close for over 25 years.

A few days later, I was watering plants on my front porch, when a butterfly landed on the top of my right hand. It stayed there for over five minutes, as I continued to walk around the porch tending to the plants. It was indeed a case of an animal or creature acting strangely. For the two days prior to the butterfly experience, I found a bird feather on my front sidewalk and one on each of the following days for about 10 days. I frequently think of Stacy as I take care of my flower gardens and I feel her spirit nearby. She had a very easy and loving relationship with things that grow in soil; it seems so natural that her spirit would come to me in nature.

I think she initially came in spirit, to thank me for a letter I wrote to her oldest son about our relationship. I sent him a copy of the few pictures I have of Stacy, along with my condolences and love to her family.

16

ROCK ME ON THE WATER

Since the passing of my friend Stacy, or at least since I became aware of it, I have found a bird feather nearly every day. I suspected from the first day that it might be spirit communication and it also seemed likely that Stacy's spirit was behind it. She was a nature lover, so any kind of small creature or reminder of them would be an appropriate way for her to try to communicate. I requested a sign from her to affirm my suspicion was correct; I asked her to leave a red feather. We have many cardinals and red finches in our area, but I had never found a red feather, before I made my request. I waited about 3 weeks and a couple of days ago my husband came in from the flower garden and handed me a red feather! I still gasp when something like that happens, even though I know to expect to receive what you ask the spirits for.
The latest surprise I received, was a small white rock that I found between the slabs of concrete of the sidewalk on the south side of my house. I water lots of plants and flowers every morning in the summer and the rock hadn't been there the day before. We don't have any of that kind of rock in our landscape and I'm not aware that any of my neighbors do either. So, if you're thinking about now: "so what's the big deal

about a rock?" let me explain further; The rock is perfectly clean and very smooth. It also has some places that shine like glitter when the sun hits them. In short, it doesn't look like a landscape rock or any other rock that's been outside for a period of time. It also looked as if it had been placed there deliberately.

As with everything I can't find an explanation for, I began to investigate; I googled this: *What does it mean if you find a small white stone?* The answer was: it can mean freedom from bondage. I found the stone right before I found out my aunt had passed away. She was suffering from Alzheimer's and now she is free. In another place it said the white stone could also mean "safe passage".

On two other occasions, I received messages that I believed were meant to tell me a loved one had passed to the next world safely. You think what you want, but I will continue to believe the signs I receive.

17

ALL MY LOVIN

When Ethan left this world, he was in the midst of raising his children. It was a role he cherished and it consumed so much of his heart, mind and soul. He was a very "hands on" father, from the moment his oldest son was born. He adored his two little boys and he was absolutely thrilled when he and Liz were told, their third child would be a girl. He wanted so much to experience fatherhood from every angle possible.

He would frequently call me late in the afternoon and I would ask him what he was doing. His reply was often, *"I'm holding a sweet little girl, while she takes her nap."* I would ask him, *"Will she wake up if you lay her down?"* and he would say, *"Maybe, but I just love to hold her and watch her sleep."*

Ethan and Liz both loved reading to their children and would take turns with each child at bedtime or sometimes, they would just talk about whatever the kids had on their minds. When Ethan was taken from his family, everything became hard, but I think bedtime was particularly hard for the kids. My grandchildren have been such a comfort to me and I have tried my best to be a comfort to them. I am so blessed to have them. Often, in talking with other parents who have lost a child, they will tell me how much they wish they could have grandchildren from the child they love and miss. I feel their pain and I understand how that would feel. I know they would willingly endure the pain I have felt, when my granddaughter cried and wanted her Daddy and it made me feel so helpless and inadequate. I often sit in an auditorium or a gymnasium and wish my grandchild could look out into the audience or up in the bleachers and see their Dad; beaming with pride. It makes one feel so powerless to know you could probably give them anything; except the one thing they so desperately want.

Ethan's daughter was five years old, when his life abruptly ended. Like so many little girls, she absolutely adored her Daddy. I remember how safe I always felt when my Daddy was nearby. Losing him at age 90, was still so painful. I miss him so much and I can't imagine having to grow up without him in my life.

On the day we had to leave Ethan at the cemetery and return home without him, reality began to set in for all of us. Later that day, my son, Jeff, wanted to return to the cemetery to change out the marker with Ethan's name on it. Because we had to deal with two mortuaries, each one had prepared a temporary marker and Jeff thought the one we had at home was nicer. It had a picture of Ethan and a short paragraph about who he was; a devoted family man and a friend to nearly everyone he ever met. When Jeff announced his decision to go back to the cemetery, nearly everyone wanted to go with him. My husband and I stayed at the house because we were exhausted and there were still people there. It was many months, before Tom would willingly go with me to the cemetery. It is still a very hard thing for him, emotionally.

It was nearly 7pm, when they arrived at the cemetery and found the gate was locked. They parked the car and climbed over the fence. They walked up to where Ethan was and as they stood there together, someone looked up and saw a pink heart-shaped balloon flying toward them. It was losing altitude and the kids began to chase it to try and catch it. It came down within the bounds of the cemetery and Ethan's son, Connor, reached up and grabbed the string that was tied to it. He gave it to Brianna. It was a "princess" balloon. Brianna was one of those little girls who loved all of the princesses. She had princess dresses, princess dolls, princess sheets, princess nightgowns etc. She believed Daddy sent her that princess balloon. She loves to do balloon launches to Daddy and often we write notes to attach to them.

Now, some would say, "Oh, you just try to make something out of everything". Picture this scene: A little girl, who's just lost the father she adores; happens to be standing beside his grave, at the very moment a pink child's balloon happens to come floating down out of the sky, to her. You can think what you will. I no longer believe in coincidence; I've seen too many things. It wasn't a red balloon that said, "Happy Birthday, Grandpa or a green balloon that said, Happy Bar Mitzvah. It was a pink princess balloon, that pretty much fell right into a little girl's hands, at a very special moment in time.

You could talk for years and never convince me; that didn't happen by design.

18

GYPSY WOMAN

*W*hen I was about 30 yrs. old, I took a position as housekeeper for the young woman and her husband who lived in the big Victorian house that Tom and I came to purchase about 20 yrs. later. I will give her a fictitious name in order to preserve the privacy of her family. I will call her Raven, because she had very dark hair and beautiful dark eyes.

Raven was an artist and designer, who worked primarily with textile arts. She was a fascinating creature and I am still amazed at the impact she had on our little town in the short time she lived there. She had an enormous impact on my life as well; though I spent only a little more than a year in her acquaintance.

Raven was unlike anyone I had ever known, or have known since. She was cheerful, funny, seemingly carefree and uniquely creative and colorful. She came to our town from a much larger city and stood out immediately. She had big plans, great ideas, lots of energy and the kind of charisma many people are drawn to; some of them, in spite of themselves. Even her husband seemed to be caught up in her charismatic energy.

I received a phone call early on a Monday morning, from

a friend who worked as a volunteer EMT with the local ambulance service. She told me she was at Raven's house and that Raven was unresponsive. She asked me if I could come there to try to calm Raven's husband down, because he was devastated. I knew her husband worked out of town and knew almost no one in the town he lived in; I had talked to him a few times on the phone, but had only spoken with him face to face once.

As I hung up the phone, I felt as if I'd been kicked in the chest. I had been at Raven's house on Friday and we had a long conversation about some changes that were going to take place with her business and that she was going to take a design job out of town. She seemed a little frustrated at this temporary derailing of her entrepreneurial plans, but I expected to return the following week and find her as cheerful as ever.

My friend, the fascinating gypsy-like Raven, passed away that morning; her heart had simply stopped and could not be restarted, no matter how many attempts were made. She was 29 yrs. old and left a five- year- old son and an adoring husband to live life without her. It was my first really close contact with tragedy and death and I was terribly ill-prepared for it.

I remained in my position as housekeeper for some time after her passing, but the house felt like a mausoleum; it seemed as if something sinister had swooped in and carried her spirit away. Raven's husband and her son spent little time there for about the first year, so the house was essentially deserted. I went every week to take care of it, just as I had before. I began to feel overwhelmed by the sadness there; it seemed as if the house and all of Raven's menagerie of animals were grieving. I started to have panic attacks, that became so intense I was put on medication for several months; still I went there every week.

One day, I was cleaning upstairs and I went into the linen room to put something away. As I turned to go back out the door, I looked down and there was a pair of Raven's sandals, that she had carelessly stepped out of and that looked to me, as if she could just walk in and slip them back on and go about her life. I suddenly felt as if someone was standing directly behind me; the sensation was so strong that I began to tremble. I knew I was alone in the house and that the doors were locked. I had an incredibly strong urge to turn around, but I was too shaken, so I just walked out the door and went downstairs to calm down. When I went back upstairs later, the sensation was gone.

This experience is still so vivid in my mind as I think of it here, while writing. Since the time of Raven's passing, I have had to deal with loss and grief many times. I was often overwhelmed by it, until I lost my own son in a shocking and tragic way and many unexplainable things began to happen. These things were amazing but not frightening. I know now that the spirit of my friend Raven was with me in that room, on that day so long ago. I regret that I was so focused on sadness, that I didn't recognize or respond to her attempt to communicate with me. Even after so many years, I am still quite emotional about Raven's loss and about what happened that day in the linen room. That is validation in my own mind, that something very significant took place.

Twenty years later, when my husband and I bought the Victorian house where Raven died, I wondered if it would bother me to live there; it didn't. Many people would ask me if the house was haunted, because at least one other person died there; I always replied: *"If it is, the spirits are friendly."*

The morning after I wrote this chapter, I turned on the television, which I rarely do at that time of day. I went to the guide to find the station I was looking for and the first thing I saw was a show called "Raven's Story". I have said this many times in my writing, but I'll say it again: *"I do not believe in coincidence!"* I know this experience was a spiritual nod from my friend, thanking me for remembering her so fondly, and for taking care of the beautiful house that was her dream also.

19

ISLE OF ST. HELENA

I hesitate to talk about dark or negative energy; it exists, but I don't believe it's what it has been represented to us as. I believe that it is a manifestation of human negativity and rumbles around in the lower reaches of human evolvement. Does this mean I don't think it is real and active on this planet? I definitely believe it exists, but the only things I'm sure of is that it was not God's creation and that we are protected from it when we realize we are children of the light and darkness cannot exist in the Presence of Light. I have experienced this dark energy on a couple of occasions and when you come face to face with it, it seems very real. I have re-written this chapter several times and thought about including it in other books, but it just doesn't seem to fit, I think it fits here, because it is an accounting of actual events in my life, and my record of personal spiritual experiences would be incomplete without it.

   This experience takes place on Halloween night in 1969; it's a night I'll never forget. Several weeks before, I had purchased a Ouija board; at that time, I believed it was just a fascinating parlor game; I soon learned otherwise.

I expected I would be spending the entire evening alone, except for my infant son, who was already asleep for the night. I received a phone call from a male relative (I think he prefers to remain nameless) who was just in town for a couple of days and asked if I wanted some company for the evening. He came over about 8:30pm and we had something to eat and just caught up on what we'd been doing since our last visit. He asked if I wanted to do anything special, since it was Halloween night and I suggested we try out the Ouija board. We set it up on a small parlor table that I moved to the center of the room; I lit a small white candle and turned off the other lights in the room. We began by asking the board several rather mundane questions; the answers were also mundane. Then we decided to really have some fun with it; I don't remember the exact way the next question was worded, but it was something like; *"Are there any spirits present?"* What happened next was pretty unnerving! There had been no answer to the question so, I suggested my companion ask the question again, still there was no answer. I was about to ask another question when I noticed my companion was acting strangely; he had lowered his head to his chest and his eyes were closed. I spoke his name, thinking he had fallen asleep in the middle of the game; he raised his head and turned to look at me. I noticed his appearance had changed to that of an older person; at the same time, I noticed the air seemed to have been vacuumed out of the room. I asked to speak to my relative; the strange visitor replied *"He isn't here."* I was beginning to be concerned and I repeated my desire to speak to my companion; the reply from the visitor was the same *"He isn't here."* I asked numerous times to speak to my relative, each time more firmly than the one before; still the visitor's reply was the same. I was really frightened by this time, and wasn't sure what I should do. I asked the visitor to tell me who he was and his only reply was nonverbal; he placed his right hand and forearm into the jacket he was wearing;(my guest for the evening wasn't wearing any kind of jacket). The gesture the visitor made immediately brought to mind Napoleon Bonaparte. I asked if my assumption was correct and he nodded in the affirmative. I was so far beyond freaked out by this time I just wanted to scream and run; but I knew it was absolutely imperative that I remain calm and continue to try to retrieve my original companion. I was beginning to think my argument wasn't working, when suddenly the visitor lowered his head to his chest and closed his eyes. I spoke the name of my guest and he raised his head, opened his eyes and appeared to have no idea what had just taken place.

It has been over 50 years since that Halloween night and my relative has consistently maintained that he has no knowledge of what happened with the Ouija board. I thought he was trying to trick me, but try as I might he still seems not to know anything about it.

I couldn't get that board out of my house fast enough; it was pitch black outside and I had no yard light to guide me down the dark sidewalk that led to the trash bin behind our garage, but I didn't care, I was more afraid of that board than I've ever been of a dark night. I didn't feel comfortable about it until the trash was picked up several days later. Since that time, I have become aware of many people advising against the use of this "game" board that was marketed as just a fun evening's entertainment. I recently read a book by a well-known medium who stated that using one of these boards is like turning on your porch light and leaving your door wide open to total strangers. I think I'd agree with that!

I encountered a similar negative force, but in a different form decades later. I recognized it from my previous experience: Early on the morning of Sept. 15, 2015, the day following the murder of my son, I lay on a sofa bed in a hotel room in Cleveland, Miss.; I was devastated at losing my youngest child in such a violent manner. I knew that without God's help I just couldn't go on. I prayed: it was a very short prayer: *Father, help me! I can't do this!"* I knew there would be an answer, but I didn't know when or in what form it would come. I believe that prayer angered whatever the negative force is that exists in this world. It suddenly entered my body in the area of my stomach and upper abdomen. It came out of nowhere, and it communicated telepathically. It began to tell me I was angry, so angry that I wanted to throw things, break things etc., but I knew there was no anger in me; there was only brokenness, disappointment and helplessness. The dark force repeatedly insisted I was violently angry and each time I rejected its negative influence, it caused me to feel a searing hot, burning pain. The repeated attacks brought to mind my experience with the Ouija board and the imperious unwanted visitor. I kept up my resistance and the beast of darkness left me as suddenly as it had come. I looked at my watch because it seemed as if this torment had gone on for many hours; over an hour had passed since the onslaught began.

   I have thought about this experience many times; each time I searched for its meaning. This is what I learned from that search: the dark beast was trying to create rage in me; it wanted to destroy my belief that God was the only one who could help me, in my despair. It was trying to convince me that it was the answer to my prayer.

   I believe this dark force visits many people in their weakest moments and causes many tragedies to occur in the world. I don't know if this force is "evil" or if it just produces evil or wicked results, but I know it's an entity that exists. I knew if I let this dark force use me to create pain and chaos, something dreadful would happen; so, I tried as hard as I could to hold it inside me. The strength I used to deny the dark beast was not my own; I had absolutely none of my own for a long period of time after my son's passing. The strength came to me from a celestial source that I can't give an exact name to; perhaps it was an angel, or it may have been Jesus; but I know it came to me and it was as real as the enemy I was wrestling with. As with the Halloween visitor, the dark beast seemed to swallow up all of the air in the room; it felt like a vacuum or void. This force only retreats when you resist it with everything in you and do it in a consistent manner. 1 Peter 5:8-9 reads: *"Be sober minded; be watchful, your adversary the devil prowls around like a roaring lion, seeking someone to devour. Resist him, firm in your faith."*

I don't believe in Satan; the little red man with the pitchfork and horns, wearing a red suit. That is a creation of men. An invisible force is much harder for humans to relate to; so, this "devil" was created to give a face to darkness. I also believe this dark force will try again to get me to do its bidding; it waits and chooses its moments carefully. When we are weakened and vulnerable it appears; I recognize it in those courtroom videos they sometimes show on the news; when a family member of a victim seems to go berserk and physically attacks the person, they believe has harmed someone they love. I've seen it when a seemingly loving father would murder his pregnant wife and little girls. It is the force responsible for pain, violence and untimely death and it feeds on the power we give it; that power makes it real. If you are visited by this dark force in the midst of pain and weakness, resist it with all the force you can. Call out the name of your God, whichever name you know him by and plead for strength to fight this darkness with the Light of Life, that it would flee and the peace of your spirit would return to you.

The Entwining

PART FOUR:
INTUITION AND ILLUMINATION

20

LADY

This is one of my earliest experiences with things that human logic can't explain; it introduced me to the fact that there is more to this world than meets the eye.

I spent most of my childhood years living in the house on Pine Street that my grandfather built, but for a few years my family lived in a much larger two-story house on Sycamore Street, in the same town. I was around 8 yrs. old when we moved to the big white house. It was there I experienced one of the first unexplainable events of my life. It happened one late summer evening, around 10 pm.

I lived in a small town and nearly every evening in the summer, there was a baseball game at the city park. Often, my brother was one of the participants and my parents would load the rest of the family in the car for an evening ride and we eventually ended up at the baseball game.

On the night this event occurred, I went to the park with my parents, but after the game ended, I asked if I could walk home. The park was about 11 blocks from our home and I assumed my parents would wait for my brother and then they would all come home together. I arrived home and found the house in complete darkness. I went inside and turned on a couple of lights downstairs and then took the front stairway up to my room. When I reached the first landing and turned to go up the next section of stairs, someone lunged at me in the dark. My heart nearly stopped before I realized it was my brother playing one of his pranks; I didn't appreciate the humor he saw in it, at all. He managed to cajole me into forgiving him fairly quickly, as usual and he suggested we go look out an upstairs window that faced the side street where you turned into our driveway, and watch for our parents to come home.

It was quite a while before our parents arrived, but we stayed at the window the whole time. A few minutes after we started watching, we saw a young woman walking up the sidewalk on the other side of the street. It was a beautiful moonlit night and we could see her quite plainly. She appeared to be formally dressed in a light blue suit; she had white gloves and shoes and carried a white purse. It was really warm that night and she looked quite overdressed for the weather. She abruptly turned up a sidewalk that led to an abandoned house; not only did no one live there, the house had been boarded up for as long as I could remember. If memory serves me right, even the front door was boarded up. We watched as the woman opened the door with no effort and walked inside, then shut the door behind her. We watched to see if a light came on, but saw nothing.

The house was a large Victorian and I know everyone thinks Victorian houses are haunted, but up to that point I wasn't aware of that. It was just odd that anyone would go there, since it had been closed up for years.

When our parents arrived home, it was getting pretty late and they made us go to bed. After they were asleep, my brother came and got me and we went back to the window to watch for the woman to come out. It's possible she left while we weren't watching, but we kept an eye on the house for days afterward and saw nothing. We were always curious as to who she was and why she went there. My brother and I thought perhaps, she was a spirit and something in me still believes that's true.

    Several years later when I was in Jr. High school, my English teacher bought the house and renovated it. I had to stop by her house one day to drop off something and she invited me in. Seeing it look so bright and comfortable on the inside, made me wonder if I really had seen what I saw that night, but I still have the same feeling about that house.

    The other mystery in this story, is how did my brother get home before I did that night; the answer is: I walked and he ran and took a shorter route. That he didn't turn on any lights, makes it seem obvious he knew I was arriving right after he did and wanted to scare the life out of me; he nearly succeeded!

21

I'VE GOT YOU UNDER MY SKIN

For most of my life, my intuition would manifest itself as a feeling of "knowing" something. I didn't think it, I "knew" it. I never really questioned how I knew; I could just feel it. One of the best examples that comes to mind is house hunting.

In 1978, Tom and I moved our family into the first home we bought as a couple. In 47 years of marriage, we have only moved 3 times. He usually lets me look first until I find something I like and then we go look at it together. Before we settled on the house we bought on Olive St., I looked at everything else in town that was available. There were a couple of places that would have met our needs; they had the right number of bedrooms and bathrooms and met our price point, but I felt lukewarm about them and hoped to find something I felt a bit more inspired about.

I reluctantly agreed to look at the Olive St. house, mostly to please the realtor; it was the one she wanted me to look at first. I have wished for years that I had taken pictures of the house as it looked the first time I saw it. It had green carpet, that looked exactly like "Astro Turf" in nearly all of the downstairs, that had been there for over 40 years. The living room had red and white flocked wallpaper with a huge design in it and the curtains were black orchard cloth with gigantic white lilies all over them. In spite of the way the house looked that day, it somehow touched my spirit; it embraced me and I knew in an instant it was the right house.

Tom and I jumped into an almost limitless round of repairs and remodeling. When the sewer backed up and had to be dug out the first week we lived there, I wondered if I'd made the right decision. Tom stripped all of the seven layers of paint off of the woodwork and stairway and we replaced the carpet, the wallpaper and the drapes. It was an amazing transformation.

We lived in that house for 23 years; the entire period that we were raising our children. When we began to think about them getting married and coming home to visit with their families, we knew the house was too small. I felt a bit sad to be leaving it, but I hoped the next owner would love it as we had and take good care of it.

I didn't have the same overwhelming sense of intuition about the big Victorian house Tom and I bought next, also in my home town. I had worked there as the cleaning lady for nearly 20 years, in an on and off fashion, so I already had a hands-on relationship with it. When we made an offer to buy it, the house wasn't on the market. I knew the owners had tried to sell it once before and decided against it, so I took a chance and asked if they'd reconsider selling it. Tom agreed to buy the house without ever seeing all of it. He had been inside as far as the front parlor on one previous occasion, but he trusted my instincts about it and we made an offer. The house always embraced me and it was our dream home for 17 yrs., but after Ethan's life was taken the dream was gone. We needed to move to be close to Ethan's wife and children, who were moving back to northeast Kansas.

I have written about the experience of finding our new home

in other books; in case you haven't read about it, I'll briefly tell you what happened. We had just looked at another house close by and as we were leaving, we drove about a block and saw a "for sale" sign, that had only been in the yard for half an hour. When I looked at the house the first time, I knew immediately it was the right place for us. I wanted to live in a parsonage; I was looking for a sanctuary and that seemed right to me. I thought the first house was my opportunity to do that and I didn't want to give up that idea. When the woman who showed me the house, told me it had been the parsonage for the old Methodist church that stood next door, I knew the spirit had led us there.

Our new home is a Queen Anne Victorian cottage and it has much the same feel and personality as the big Queen Anne we moved from. I use the word personality because I believe houses have distinct personalities; it might be more accurate to say they have a spirit. If you're wondering how a house can have a spirit; let me explain.

Most houses are made of wood or at least some elements are wood; wood comes from trees. Trees were once a living thing and every living thing has a God-given spirit. It is not an advanced spirit like humans have, but it is spirit nevertheless. It is this spirit that talks to me and lets me know I've found the right place for us to live.

Olive St. House – First house Tom and I purchased; where our children grew up.

My favorite photo of 404 N Walnut St.

22

I SAW THE LIGHT

*B*efore Tom and I moved to our Queen Anne cottage, we lived in a much bigger Queen Anne Victorian. Our former home had several beautiful stained-glass windows; it was one of the things we loved about the house. At certain times of day, if the sun was in the right position, the prism in the stained-glass panel in the top portion of the window in the front parlor, would shoot beautiful little rainbows all over the floor of the room.

When we moved from the large Queen Anne, we both missed the stained-glass pieces and the rainbows. Tom began buying stained glass pieces that had been salvaged from old homes and churches, to hang as inserts in the windows of our new home. We have them in nearly every room now. It is so lovely to see the light hitting them in the morning when I open my eyes. They are so much more beautiful when they are illuminated, as it is with our spirits.

As a small child, I was fascinated with kaleidoscopes; they were an inexpensive toy you could buy in "Five and Dime" department stores. A kaleidoscope consists of a cardboard tube with two mirrors and confetti, or small colored stone chips inside that move when you turn the tube. If you hold it up to the light, the shifting patterns it makes become illuminated, which makes the designs even more beautiful.

I have always loved Christmas trees, in fact, I love them so much that I have a small illuminated tree in the corner of my TV room, that stays lit all year; I just change out the decorations to fit the season. After Christmas, it becomes a Valentine tree and then a St. Patrick's Day tree and so on throughout the year. I love all of the different manifestations of my little tree, but it would be nothing without the illumination from the tiny white lights.

For many years, I was a professional seamstress, and during that time I made nearly everything that can be made from fabric. Of all of the things I made, wedding gowns were what I loved most. Those gowns took many hours to create, many of the pieces were adorned with sequins and beads; all of which I hand sewed onto the gowns. One dress had over seven thousand sequins, crystal beads and pearls sewn onto it. As beautiful as the gowns were, they were never complete until you put them on the bride and the glow from her face, the soft lights and the candles hit all of those beads and sequins. The dress became almost a living thing. The inner glow of the bride's happy spirit, implanted by God, was the beautiful finishing touch that every eye beheld as she moved down the aisle to be joined in marriage.

One day several years ago, my daughter-in-law Carol and I attended a celebration of "World Day of Prayer". As we strolled the beautiful grounds outside, after the ceremony was over, I noticed a woman standing across from me; I couldn't take my eyes off of her; something beautiful radiated from inside her. She was literally glowing from the inside to the outside of her physical being; I had never seen anything like that. I believe she was the first truly illuminated spirit I ever saw

This chapter is obviously about illumination and if you've never been fortunate enough to observe the glow of an illuminated spirit, I can tell you it is a mesmerizing experience. Have you ever watched a small child when they are in the presence of a glowing candle or fire light? They are totally mesmerized by the illumination; they want to move closer; they want to touch the glowing light they see before them. I want to reach that state of illumination in my own spiritual journey; that has become my goal in life.

"This is the message we have heard from Him and we declare to you, that God is light and in Him there is no darkness at all."
1 John 1:15

"For you were once darkness, but now you are light in the Lord. Walk as children of light"
Ephesians 5:8

"Let your light so shine before men that they may see your good works and glorify your Father in heaven."
Matthew 5:16

The illuminating event I want to relate now, occurred about 3-4 weeks after Ethan's passing. During that time, I had been unable to look at pictures of my son, because they caused me nearly unbearable pain. I didn't put them away, but I avoided looking at them. It is only in the last few months, that I have tied that experience and the one I'm going to relate here, together. I don't know why, I didn't see it before, but it took me years to make the connection.

One morning, as I stood at my kitchen sink washing some

dishes, I looked over my shoulder into the dining room. On the antique buffet that belonged to Tom's maternal grandmother, was a picture of Ethan and his family. If you were standing directly in front of the picture you would see Ethan's image in the lower righthand corner; his wife, Liz is standing in back of him, at his left shoulder. In the upper left-hand corner are their three children grouped together. As I looked at the picture that day, I saw a perfect oval of golden light hitting Ethan's image; it was only Ethan's image that was being illuminated. I couldn't imagine where the light was coming from; the room is normally quite dark and the drapes were closed. I looked to the south end of the house at the stained glass I described earlier in this chapter (in the top of the large window at the end of the front parlor). The beam of light was coming from the prism in the center of the stained-glass panel. I'm not sure that was even possible, but if it was, several things would have to align in order for it to occur.

First, the sun would have to be in exactly the right location. Then, the light from the sun would have to filter through the leaves on the huge old elm tree that stood in the south end of the yard. It would have to hit the prism in the exact spot it did in order to shoot a beam of light through the parlor, the foyer and to the end of the dining room, where the picture stood on the buffet; a distance of nearly fifty feet. The beam of light would have to bend slightly to the left in order to illuminate Ethan's image.

At the beginning of this story, I mentioned that the prisms in the stained-glass panel created rainbows when the afternoon sun hit them. Over the course of the 17 years we lived in the house and the nearly twenty years I worked in the house prior to buying it, I never, not once, saw a single-colored beam of light that shot all the way to the other end of the house. In fact, the rainbows never went farther than the end of the parlor floor, where it joined the parquet floor of the foyer. I never saw a single beam of light other than on the day I observed it on Ethan's image.

I continued to watch the picture for months and the beam of light never appeared again.

There are a couple of things I find amazing about this story: First, is the fact that I was in the exact right place to see it, at the time it occurred; the illumination only lasted about ten minutes. Perhaps, the most amazing thing was that after the illumination, I was able to look at Ethan's pictures without the intense pain I had experienced before this occurred.

This illumination clearly fits the definition of a miracle; so many unlikely things had to come together in order for it to occur. When I came to the realization that this was nearly impossible, I got chills. I never even considered believing it was a coincidence and I know I didn't imagine the impossible for a full ten minutes.

Outside picture of the South end of our house on Walnut St. You can see some of the branches of the large elm tree that shaded most of the South yard. The stained glass with the prism that sent the beam of light onto Ethan's picture is on the left (in the bay).

This is the front parlor and shows the prism in the stained glass panel. The buffet where Ethan's family picture was sitting, was at the opposite end of the house.

Ethan's Family – This is the picture that was illuminated by a beam of golden light.

23

PRECIOUS ANGEL / SHINE YOUR LIGHT

I received a calling to my spirit to share my story, about six months after Ethan's life was taken. This calling is not only to share the tragedy of our loss, but most importantly to share the positive spiritual message of healing and peace that it precipitated in my life. I am called to share complete Truth, and my experience of the Light as well as the darkness; evil. I hesitate to use that word, because it generates an impression the world believes is accurate and causes fear and anxiety. It impedes a more rational and spiritual view of what darkness really is and where it originates. I don't have all of the answers and I don't claim to; what I do have is my own experiences with it. I share them with you here in order to create a complete record of what happened in my life and to demonstrate the pattern I have observed in my experiences with darkness.

The pattern I speak of, is outlined in the story of the "temptation of Jesus", found in Matthew, Mark and Luke in the Holy Bible. While the story raises many questions, it also declares one very important point: When Satan(darkness) left Jesus, it was only to lay in wait for another opportunity to come back and try once more to tempt him. Darkness feels more like a force or an essence, instead of a person or a form; though I believe it can take whatever form it needs to, in order to get what it wants. I have experienced this pattern with it numerous times in my life; though before Ethan passed, I didn't recognize it as such.

Most of us underestimate the power of negativity (darkness) to seep insidiously into our thoughts and once allowed a voice, to influence our actions. I used to listen to that negative voice a lot and its influence always brought trouble, pain and confusion. It was the source of my doubts about my own worthiness; my value as a human being. It was directly responsible for the inferiority complex I lived with for the first 30 yrs. of my life.

When I wanted to get married, at 17 years of age, it was the voice which insisted, that was a reasonable decision and gave me the false confidence to think I could make that work. It told me I was mature enough and had reached a point where I was going to be who I was in that moment, forever. It told me I was fully accomplished as the person I was destined to become. Now I see the error of that idea, because as part of creation, which is ever evolving, we too are ever changing; God is never finished with us.

That negative voice caused me to suffer depression, to the point where I seriously considered suicide. The dark voice told me I wasn't good enough, smart enough or capable enough. It is a paralyzing influence and it will seek any opportune moment of weakness to be heard.

When I stay in my spiritual space or consciousness, I am invulnerable to its influence. Staying in full consciousness is hard, while living in the world. It tries to pull you out of your spiritual space of peace and strength. I am at my best these days when I maintain my consciousness. The pandemic has made that easier to do, but as things open up and people are going more and doing more, it becomes harder to maintain it. I still live in this world and it isn't possible to avoid being out in it totally, but sometimes I remind myself of the scripture about the "armor of God" found in Ephesians 6:10-18. Even knowing we are protected, I am still most comfortable in my old- fashioned cottage, that I call home now. I also know that sometimes, the safest place for us isn't in this world.

"Put on the whole armor of God, that ye may be able to withstand the wiles of the devil.
For we wrestle not against flesh and blood, but against principalities, against powers, against the rulers of the darkness of this world, against spiritual wickedness in high places. Wherefore take unto you the whole armor of God, that you may be able to stand in the evil day and having done all, to stand."
Ephesians 6:11-18

24

CANDLE IN THE WIND

It seems so natural to us that we will one day sit beside our aging parents as they complete their earthly journey; that is not to say it is an easy or desirable thing to do. When my father's mother passed, it was as if he no longer had a rudder to help him steer his life's ship. This was in spite of the fact that it had been many years since she had been involved in the decisions he made for his life. I recognized that feeling when my father passed; that feeling of suddenly being set adrift without the protection of a security device: no life jacket or life preserver. If we have good and loving parents, they loosen their control over us when the time is right, but they hover somewhere in the distance, always ready to step into our lives in time of need.

When I look back at my father's passing, there are two things that stand out in my mind; the first, I marveled at on that day and ever since, the second thing only became apparent with the passage of some time. I have written about them both before; they are part of my spiritual story and so I repeat them here.

In March of 2015, my father was in the last stages of Alzheimer's and living in a nursing home that was about 20 miles from where I and my sister lived at that time. We visited him as often as we could, and some days his eyes still lit up when he saw us coming down the hall toward him; other times he seemed not to know exactly who we were.

We received a call from my father's second wife that he was being placed in the care of hospice; they would come in and supervise his care, but he would remain in the same facility. We were told he was in the last two weeks of his life; he was 90 years old at that time. Soon after this news, we received another call that informed us that if we wanted to see him before he passed, we should come very soon. Jeanne and I and our brother Layne, went and sat with him all through the afternoon and evening and well into the night. The nursing staff suggested it would be fine for us to go home at that point, because they weren't seeing anything that indicated his passing was imminent. We returned the next day and he was sitting in the dining room at the table, eagerly awaiting his lunch. He lived another 9 months before we received another call to come right away if we wanted to be with him when he passed. We repeated the same vigil as before; we sat next to his bed all afternoon and late into the night.

My father was a musician and we played soft music in the background; mostly violins and dulcimers, which he loved. Even though he appeared to be in a semi-comatose state, he would tap his toes in time to the music. He seemed quite relaxed.

In spite of having been a lay minister for many years, he had an intense fear of death, but as we had observed with our mother as she lay dying of cancer 13 years earlier, a gentle peace settled over him in his last hours. We left his room for no longer than ten minutes and when we returned, the hospice nurse met us at the door of his room and told us he had passed five minutes earlier. When we reentered the room, he had already been prepared for the mortuary team to take him. He had an ever so slight smile on his lips and his body seemed to be glowing, as if it were lit from within. He looked peaceful; it was beautiful and amazing.

The second significant thing about my father's passing is that I began to mourn his loss long before he actually passed. On the day in March, when we received the first phone call that told us he would soon pass; I wrote his eulogy late that night before I went to bed, only to find him up and dressed and ready for lunch the next day. I still believed his death was imminent and I cried every night for months at the thought of him passing from my life; that did not end until my son was murdered on the 14th of September. I will always believe there was Divine intervention at work during that period of time. Had I not mourned for my father early, I would have been unable to do so at all, because at the time he passed, I was consumed with grief at the murder of my son. I had lived for thirteen years with regret that when my mother passed, I was so numb that I couldn't even cry for her. I didn't want it to be like that when my father passed, 3 months after my son.

Grief is hard and it hurts, but even as it hurts, it is also allowing us to heal. I will never forget the heavenly light that lit my father's countenance, as he made his way to his heavenly home.

25

FAITHFULLY

I couldn't possibly write a book about my spiritual experiences and leave out the most transformational experience of my life. Even though I have included it in my two prior books, I just can't omit it from this one. Instead of including the chapter I wrote for "Learn to be Still", I will tell the story here in a shortened, paraphrased version.

It happened at the cemetery on the day of Ethan's Celebration of Life service, Sept. 20, 2015. At the end of the graveside service, as people moved through in front of me, to offer their condolences, I looked to my right, out from under the canopy we were seated beneath. I thought I saw someone who has been a dear friend for over 40 years. It appeared to be him at first, but then his appearance changed to that of someone I had never seen before. I knew what I was witnessing was a transfiguration, which at any previous time of my life, I would have found frightening, but as it happened that day, I remained completely calm. The figure of the unknown person was standing approximately 10-15 ft. away from me, so I could see his facial features very clearly. His eyes were the most impressive aspect of his face. They were very dark brown and so luminous, they nearly glowed; I found myself unable, or not wanting to look away from them. They were magnetic and they expressed so much to me in a very short span of time. As I gazed into them, the level of love and compassion they projected is impossible to describe with human language; I was overwhelmed. His eyes projected his thoughts toward me and at the same time I felt myself being pulled toward him, in a spiritual sense. His gaze never shifted from my face, as he imparted a telepathic message directly to my heart. He said: *"I am here. I have always been here."* Then his focus shifted to Ethan and he said: *"He's with me and he's fine. Don't worry about him."* At that point, someone stepped in front of me and I was forced to look away. When I looked back, I saw only my friend.

On the day of the transfiguration, I wasn't sure who it was that I saw and received a message from; I thought it might have been an angel, but I knew that wasn't quite right. It bothered me for months afterward, until I let myself accept the possibility that I had been looking into the eyes of Jesus. I was taught at an early age that no one would look upon Jesus until they saw him in heaven, so it didn't immediately seem rational to believe it was actually Him. Just those few words I exchanged with Him that day, changed everything for me. It changed what I believed to be true, to what I "know" is True.

26

I AM YOUR ANGEL

As I began to look back at things that happened prior to losing my son, I remembered some things that now seem to have been preparation for the tragedy that was going to occur. At the time these things were happening, I had no explanation for them. I was puzzled by them, but they didn't frighten me, they just seemed odd. There were no messages associated with them that would have led me to believe a tragedy was going to occur that would alter our lives forever.

These odd experiences were ushered in, in 2011, the year I turned 60 years old. Ethan orchestrated a surprise birthday party for me from his home in Lubbock, Texas. He enlisted the help of my sister, Jeanne and our good friend, Debra, in order to make it happen. My birthday is the 29th of August and I wasn't the least bit surprised when family members started showing up around that time, because Tom and I always had a Labor Day party for our family and extended family. I just assumed everyone was coming to be there for the Labor Day get together.

Ethan managed to pull off the surprise and I had no clue before I walked into the local bar and grill, thinking I was there to have supper, so I wouldn't have to cook for all of those people, after working at my antique store all day. I enjoyed the party, went home exhausted and fell into bed. As soon as I opened my eyes the next morning, I knew the world had shifted overnight. It felt as if someone had turned the world I knew 180 degrees, while I was sleeping. Anyone who knew me well at the time would have known that I was very sure of what I believed about nearly anything you could mention and I rarely ever changed my mind about anything. When I woke that morning, I realized I felt differently about a lot of things. I wondered to myself, if everyone who turns 60 has a revelation like that?

Some of the things that had changed were community service projects I had been involved with. I was creator and director of two of them and had been elected president of another. All of these things occupied a great deal of my time and thought. I know now I was being guided to get out of these things; I had no idea why, but I didn't question it. Over the next few months, I handed over the reins of all of these projects to other people. My guidance indicated I was to stay home, shut the door and nurture my own spirit. I proceeded to do just that for four years. During that time, another strange thing began to happen. I would wake up between 3am and 3:30, with the awareness that something had been hovering over me just as I opened my eyes, but then it disappeared. I sensed it more than saw it. I don't know why I didn't find this frightening, but I was just puzzled by it. This occurred at least 3 times, that I have very distinct memories of. Then came the day shortly after my 64th birthday (August 29,2015) that I received the phone call that informed me my son, Ethan had been murdered; I knew in an instant my life would never be the same.

When I had the experience of waking to find something was hovering over me, I had been sleeping deeply and I was in a darkened room. My memory is that there were two "beings" hovering about 2-3 ft. above me. They appeared dark, probably because the room itself was dark. They were covered with some type of gauzy looking fabric that swirled, as if it was being blown by the wind. They did not seem threatening or ominous in any way. Instead, they seemed to be communicating concern to each other; I assumed their concern was for me. I was disappointed that each time, as soon as they became aware that I was awake, they disappeared. I have always believed they were guardians, perhaps angels, though they didn't appear in a form that others have reported when having been visited by angelic beings. I believe they were there to prepare me in some way for the tragedy that was going to occur, perhaps to somehow help me survive the unthinkable loss of my son. I have never been aware of their presence since that awful day, when Ethan's life was taken.

I now see several ways I was being prepared for what happened to Ethan. That tells me nothing on earth happens without higher knowledge and preparation and that preparation involves varying facets of spiritual presence.

I have felt guidance every step of the way, as I struggled to find my way out of staggering grief and find a pathway to a life I felt was worth living. I am guided to write and write and write. I am guided to share my story of grief and gratitude. Each time I follow this guidance I am showered with new blessings of joy and peace.

The Entwining

A Journey of Transformation

PART FIVE: RECURRING THOUGHTS AND FEELINGS

27

REACH OUT I'LL BE THERE

On Sept. 27, 2020, Ethan would have celebrated his 45th birthday; we celebrated without him here. About that time, I began to recognize I was having a recurring thought about contacting the mother of the person responsible for Ethan's passing. I wanted to tell her I have forgiven her son for what happened. I forgave him about 6 months after Ethan's life was taken, but it has taken me this long to arrive at the point where I was able to reach out to her.

I never ignore my recurring thoughts; they are nearly always guidance from the Holy Spirit. I knew it might be difficult to find the family I was looking for, because I only had a last name and the city where they resided 6yrs. ago. Jeanne and I both began to search the internet to find them. I was able to find the name and address of someone I hoped was a brother, another son, of the woman I was looking to find. I wrote the mother a letter, wrote a cover letter explaining who I was, and why I wanted to contact the family, and sent the letter to the brother of Ethan's assailant. On the day I mailed it, something unexpected happened.

As I was looking online for the address I needed, I came across a newspaper article from the time surrounding the horrific event that took Ethan from us. I was shocked to see pictures of a professional cleaning service, removing carpet from Ethan's office. The pictures weren't graphic, but it was obvious what was being cleaned up; the aftermath of a tragedy, our tragedy. I was horrified, I never knew those pictures existed and I couldn't understand why they were taken, or why anyone felt it necessary to publish them. They were an appalling invasion of Ethan's privacy and ours as well. The pictures upset me so much, I was shaking violently from head to toe. The peace Jesus planted in my heart following the murder of my son, isn't easily disturbed, but on the day I saw those pictures, I couldn't regain my sense of well-being or the calmness of my spirit.

When the news article that contained the pictures came up on my computer, the screen was divided. On the other side of the screen was a picture of the note of apology Shannon wrote and left at the home of his fiancée, who's life he took the day before he took Ethan's. The note was written before Ethan's life ended and there was no mention of him in it. Shannon never mentioned Ethan at all, not even to the police who talked to him by phone, while he was on the run; he seemed not to care about what he had done to my son. When I saw the note on my screen, I initially ignored it; I had read it before. I was totally focused on those reprehensible pictures.

On the day I was prepared to mail my letter to Shannon's family, I planned to drop it by the mail box and then proceed to Lawrence, where I had errands to take care of. As I was about to drop the letter in the mail slot, I hesitated. I thought about what I was doing for a couple of long drawn- out minutes and then let it go. I got back in my car and headed out of town on the back road.

I began to see those awful, hurtful pictures in my mind and

I began to shake all over again, but suddenly the image of the note of apology popped into my mind. I read it again, but this time I sensed it was being presented spiritually, as an apology to me, from Shannon. My attitude about it was instantly changed; here was the apology we never received from him. My peace and calm were restored within a short time of the presentation, and my acceptance, of the apology the note represented.

When I decided to write the letter to Shannon's family, I was hoping to receive a response, but I knew it was likely there would be none. I waited about a week and suddenly there was an email on my phone, from the man I sent the letter to. My assumption had been right, he was Shannon's brother. He told me he had given the letter to his mother and that I would probably hear from her soon.

A week passed after I received the email and I began to believe I would never hear from Shannon's mother. The "still small voice" that is my spiritual guidance, kept saying: *"Be patient"*. I knew if I never received a response to my letter, I would be alright, because I had done what the "voice" repeatedly urged me to do.

When we forgive, it is a two-step process. The recognition within ourselves that forgiveness has taken place, lifts a burden we have carried. Announcing that forgiveness is given, lifts a burden from someone else. The universe is purified in some way, when both of these things happen.

About the time I decided an answer wasn't coming, I received an email from Shannon's mother. She thanked me for the letter and expressed concern for my grandchildren. She said she had thought of me often. She told me she loves her son and that he had suffered a nervous breakdown and had been on some very strong prescription medications. It was the only foreign substance found in his body at the time of the autopsy, that was performed after he ended his own life. His mother believes it was the medication that led to the terrible tragedy that took three lives and broke so many hearts. I have always believed Shannon wasn't himself when he committed these acts; those who knew him well, say they were totally out of character for the person they knew him to be.

Since I sent the letter and received a reply to it, I am at peace knowing I forgave him and that his mother is aware that I did. I thought of her often as I tried to bring myself to forgive Shannon's actions, that had broken my heart. I knew that if anyone was suffering more than we were, it had to be his mother; we were dealing with one tremendous loss, she was trying to make sense of the loss of three lives, while trying to accept that the son she loved so much, had caused such unspeakable grief to so many people.

Because I sent the letter, I had the experience of discovering those very disturbing pictures, but I also feel like Shannon touched my spirit and offered his regret for taking Ethan's precious life; so, the good outweighs the bad. I have learned through the tragedy of Ethan's loss that God can and does take the worst things that happen and transforms them, so that something good can come from them. It is a healing process and it's one I feel we are supposed to adopt and apply ourselves, as we strive to heal our broken world.

28

SMOKE GETS IN YOUR EYES

*A*bout January of this year (2021) I began to smell cigarette smoke nearly every evening. I have found no explanation for this experience, even though I have tried pretty hard to figure it out. I don't immediately decide something unusual is spiritual unless I recognize the spirit who is responsible, or unless I can find no other explanation. Once I have decided spirit is involved, I try to determine who the spirit could be, why they wish to make themselves known and what message they are trying to convey.

   I began to suspect spirit was involved in the cigarette smoke experience, because neither my husband or I smoke and no one else smokes in our home. When I would smell the smoke, I would check everything in the house, such as the stove or the furnace etc. I then would go outside and look around to see if there was anyone using a backyard smoker for meat, or if they had a firepit burning. I even wondered if the city's burn pit was smoking. I could find absolutely no source for the smell of smoke in my house. The odor was very strong, so strong it sometimes made me cough and my eyes watered. It is strongest around the recliner I sit in every evening.

   Only on one previous occasion have I ever been visited by a

spirit that was not known to me; someone I knew in this life. I am usually able to determine the identity of the visitor pretty quickly, but this time I was a bit puzzled. I came up with four possibilities: My Aunt Anna, her husband Richie, our neighbor on Pine St., Helen, and my father-in-law, Don. I narrowed it down to Uncle Richie, based on the fact that I had recently mentioned him in the book I was writing, his name also came up in a recent conversation I was having with my sister, regarding a scale model oil derrick Richie had made many years ago. I also had written a chapter about my friend Karen and I spending a lot of time at his workshop, listening to the radio and learning to dance. All of these things happened in the week before I began to smell cigarette smoke.

Uncle Richie isn't someone I think about real often; he passed away in the early 1960's and I was 14 yrs. old at that time. The last couple of years of his life, I didn't see him much; I was unhappy with him about something and I didn't go to see him. When I finally did, he was dying and I was afraid to go close enough to speak to him. I didn't think he probably knew I was even there. I have previously mentioned in my books that I had a very unforgiving nature for many years. I began to suspect these visitations had something to do with hard feelings and unfinished business.

Part of the work of a" life review" is recognizing your mistakes and forgiving others for theirs. Holding grudges gets in the way of spiritual growth. As I work my way through this life review, there are other people and situations that come to mind, in which I know I have unresolved issues. I hadn't thought about Uncle Richie being one of those people, until I suspected this sudden sense of burning cigarettes might be his spirit trying to get my attention. I, like most people believed that after someone passes out of this world, it is too late to rectify unfinished or unresolved issues with them.

Uncle Richie was a very talented man, he could make many things, repair lots of things, create things, write philosophical essays on such subjects as death, etc. He was a pretty temperamental person and was easily angered. In the context of card playing, which he often did, he was a person who always played to win. He would sometimes play little mind games with you, which was something I didn't appreciate much. He lost his father at a very young age and was raised by his widowed mother. He had a sister who was blind and he became responsible for them early in his life. His personality (spirit) was complex and could be difficult or funny and generous. As long as I knew him, he smoked unfiltered Camel cigarettes almost continuously; it was a very strong odor, one that I easily recognize to this day.

One afternoon, I sat down and had a conversation with him; I talked, and I'm pretty sure he was listening. I explained that I was sorry for not being around the last couple of years of his earthly life and also sorry if I had misunderstood his intentions. I told him I appreciated all of the nice things he had done for me, my siblings and friends. I also said I have no lingering bad feelings toward him and I hope his spirit finds peace and blessing in that knowledge.

The smell of smoke didn't completely disappear after I spoke with Uncle Richie, but it doesn't show up as much as it did. There is still no other explanation for this occurrence, but I'm keeping an open mind.

29

LAY DOWN BESIDE ME

Ethan was always a very affectionate child and that didn't change as he became an adult and moved hundreds of miles from home. He had a habit of reaching out and holding my hand, nearly every time we sat next to each other. When he was little, he watched "Gilligan's Island" every afternoon; he always wanted me to sit beside him in our big blue rocking chair and watch it too! He liked to sit beside me on the sofa and hold my hand while he told me everything he had on his mind. The last time I was in his home in Mississippi, he sat with me on the sofa and held my hand; he was nearly 40 years old. He told me how much he loved his family and his teaching career and writing books. He told me about the books he wanted to write in the future. Those memories come flooding back whenever I sit beside Ethan's oldest son, Connor, and he absentmindedly reaches out to hold my hand. I always feel Ethan's presence when that happens and it happens often when Connor sits close to me.

After Ethan's passing, I would ask him to hold my hand when I was really struggling with grief and it would bring his spirit very close to me. Sometimes, I wake up in the night because I feel the bed move, as if someone has just sat down on the edge of it, or as if someone laid down next to me. I remember a couple of times before Ethan left us, when he had come to visit and came into my room to see if I was awake. If I was, he would lay down on the covers beside me and we would have a long talk.

I have also had experiences during the night when I would wake up because I felt a small hand pat my leg; I remember that sensation from when my kids were little. One such occasion was around Christmas 2020; I am never afraid when these things happen, because I know what it is and who it is. I awoke early on Christmas Day 2019, when I heard a child's voice say: *"Mom?"* as if he needed me to do something. Christmas has always been a time of heightened emotion for me and it is much more so since losing my son. It is a time I am more likely to hear Ethan speak to me or to receive a spontaneous sign from him. Mother's Day is the same; there is usually a sign or message of some kind. Last year around my birthday, I was looking for something I hadn't been able to find since our last move. I found a box in the upstairs guest room that I hadn't unpacked, because I knew I had no place to put what was in it. I found what I was looking for, but there was a lovely surprise too; it was the last birthday card Ethan sent me in 2015, 2 weeks before he passed. It is a beautiful, sentimental card, with a beautiful message and he signed it with love. I knew it was the last birthday card, because many years ago I began dating the special cards I received. I have books full of them and they make me happy, sad, grateful and emotional each time I look through them. Signs like these are so comforting and I feel so blessed each time I recognize one.

30

MAMA

I had my children early in life; the first just before I turned eighteen; the second at nearly twenty and the last at twenty-three. Having children was really the only clearly-defined goal I ever set for myself. In my youthful exuberance, I thought I wanted at least five children; the experience of Ethan's birth convinced me it would be foolish to press my luck any further; at that point, three seemed like the right number.

Once I discovered I was physically capable of having children, I took it for granted for many years after I decided not to have anymore; just knowing that I could if I wanted to, was enough for me. Time passed, as it does for all of us and the day came when my body let it be known that my ability to give birth was no longer there. It came as something of a shock, even though it had been many years since I had given any serious thought to having more children. It was a loss I mourned, much to my amazement. I thought I'd be happy when I reached the point of not having to deal with monthly periods and I certainly didn't miss that part of it, but I guess I felt like my life's purpose had abandoned me. I adjusted to the loss and gave it little thought until Ethan's passing.

While my husband and I, along with our son Jeff, were in

Mississippi following the tragedy that took Ethan from us, Jeff overheard a conversation between our daughter-in-law and a well-intentioned friend. She said to Ethan's wife, Liz: *"Don't let these people push you around; they're just his parents; You're the wife!"* It was the second very significant time in my life that someone who didn't even know me, presumed to know what kind of relationship I had with a daughter-in-law, and it hurt just as much as the first time it happened. In that case, it made me extremely angry; in this case, I was beyond anger; I didn't have anything left inside to be angry with. I was devastated, broken beyond words. I thought to myself: *"My daughter-in-law is a young woman, she can have another husband someday, if she chooses that; but I can never have another child, and if I could, it would be just that, "another child". It wouldn't be Ethan.*

In the first book I wrote, "Learn To Be Still", I talked about two images that came to my mind repeatedly, after Ethan's passing; one was a visual memory and the other was so incredibly tactile that I actually could feel it. I relived many times the first moments I held Ethan in my arms, following his birth. I could feel the weight of his body in my arms and how it felt to touch him, as I patted his back, while I held him up to my shoulder and nuzzled his tiny cheek next to mine. I remembered the first words I ever spoke to him: *"Hello Ethan, I'm your Mama, and I love you."*

Tonight, as I thought of him, nearly six years since he was taken from me, I had that sensation again, exactly as it was before; how sweet it was to have that experience again. Earlier today, as I looked through my cedar chest for something that belonged to my dad, I saw Ethan's baby clothes, that I had kept for so many years; two little pairs of poplin overalls and two tiny flannel shirts. They were a gift from Tom's sister, Barbara, and I loved them so much I just had to keep them. When I saw them today, I lovingly touched them, as thoughts of him wearing them floated through my mind. I know it was this memory that triggered the amazing sensation of holding him in my arms one more time. I am so blessed!

The Entwining

PART SIX: VISIONS

31

VISIONS OF JOHANNA

One of the few spiritual experiences I've had that makes me a little uncomfortable is visions. It isn't that they are inherently negative, because they are usually a warning about something that is about to occur and that has sometimes, been a benefit. I'm pretty sure if I stopped trying to block them, they would occur more often, but I'm not sure I'd like that. I don't want to know what will happen in the future if it's something bad, because I might be powerless to prevent it and I usually don't get a lot of details with the visions. I don't know when or where or to whom the event will happen.

The visions I have are very brief, just glimpses of something and then it's gone. I see them clearly and they are in color. In one of them, the person who appeared spoke to me. As I began thinking about writing this chapter, I remembered another vision that happened about 20 years ago that I hadn't thought of in all those years and I saw it as an unrelated incident; now I see it in the same way I look at the more recent visions.

In 2000, my husband and I purchased a big Victorian house. It belonged to friends of mine, who I had worked for as a housekeeper for about 20 years, so I had a very hands on experience with the house before I ever lived there. On the day we were moving in, my mother had a doctor's appointment in a neighboring town. I was unable to go, but my sister Jeanne took her. About the middle of the afternoon, I went outside to get something out of my car and saw Jeanne walking toward me in the gravel driveway of the new house. I asked how the appointment had gone and she told me our mother had just been told she had cancer in her bladder, which had already perforated into her abdominal cavity. At the exact moment Jeanne said the word cancer, I had a vision of my mother in a dark colored casket, wearing the red suit she owned. Red was her favorite color and I thought the suit looked so good on her; that's the only explanation for the clothes she was wearing in the vision. I tried to shake the vision off as just a reaction to the shock of finding out my mother was seriously ill, but it foretold the future. My mother passed from cancer in January of 2002; she was buried in a blue casket and a costume she wore when performing. Even though the imagery in the vision was incorrect, the future it presented was accurate.

The next vision I had occurred after Ethan's passing. I was preparing to move out of the big Victorian we had been in for 17 years, and that meant a lot of sorting through and ridding myself of unnecessary things; we were moving into a much smaller house. I found an old picture of my mother's Uncle Richie's family; I don't remember ever seeing the picture before that day. We discovered one of his uncles was buried in our local cemetery and Jeanne and I decided to see if we could find a grave marker for him. He was in the directory, but there was no stone.

Ten days prior to finding the picture and searching for "Uncle Alfred's" grave, I had another snapshot vision; this time it was a hideous looking reptile, the long skinny kind that slithers. I have always been terrified of such creatures and even saying the word can cause nightmares.

So, Jeanne and I were at the cemetery walking around, looking for a stone with Alfred's name on it. As I walked past a long flat mottled looking stone, I turned around and looked down, curled up on the stone was the hideous viper in my vision. Needless to say, our search ended abruptly!

A few weeks later, I had another vision: This time I was driving and a blue truck pulled out in front of me and I nearly hit it. I told Jeanne about each of these visions as they occurred, and we discussed the blue truck vision. Again, about 10 days later, Jeanne and I were in my car and as I pulled out onto the highway she screamed, as a blue car I nearly turned into, went past us on the passenger side. I always look more than once before I pull out onto a highway and I did so on that day; I can't explain how I didn't see the blue car. The vision wasn't exactly accurate in detail; it was a blue car, not a blue truck and I pulled out in front of the car, not the other way, as in the vision, but it was a warning none-the-less.

The next vision I had was of a little boy with dark eyes and very dark hair; again, it was just a flash and it was gone. The boy said *"My name is Adam."* That was all! I believe Adam is the child I lost in a miscarriage; it is the only connection I can identify. I was puzzled because of the dark hair and eyes; my other sons were all blonde haired as young children and had blue or green eyes.

One morning, I woke and sat up on the edge of my bed, I suddenly noticed the picture of me as a one-year-old, that hangs on the wall next to my closet door; I saw a young child with very dark eyes and dark hair. I was also puzzled by the name "Adam", because I don't think I would have picked it for my child. I have wondered if the name represents "firstborn", because that would be my miscarried child's place in birth order. Biblically, Adam was thought to be the first man.

The visions quieted down for a few years until a couple of

months ago; I had a vision of a fender bender type car accident. All I could see was a dark colored car with fender damage. I warned my husband, who currently drives a black Cadillac, to be careful, because I'd had a vision of an accident. He doesn't take some of these things real seriously, but I did tell him about it. I also mentioned it to my sister.

About a week after I had the vision, my husband and I were in the doctor's office and his phone rang. It was my daughter-in-law and she told us our grandson had just had a fender bender in the next town; he was driving his black Honda Accord.

Many people have visions, but a lot of people ignore them or dismiss them; I have learned to pay attention to them the same way I pay attention to and often act on recurring thoughts. The universe is trying to connect with us all the time and it may be quite important to pay attention to the messages you receive.

My baby picture – In the vision of Adam that flashed before my eyes, I saw a child with dark hair and dark eyes, then I realized that was just like me.

32

ANGEL EYES

I became fully aware of my angels, after Ethan's passing. I feel them beside me and sometimes slightly behind me, but even when I don't feel them, I know they are there. I often ask them to go with me when I leave my house; especially when I am going on a road trip, or away from home for a lengthy period of time. I ask them to surround my car if I'm driving, or to fly beside the plane, if I am traveling by air.

A few days ago, I met my sister in a place that's about halfway between her home and mine. We picked up lunch and sat in a park to visit for a few hours. I haven't been able to see her much since the Covid shut down. We had a wonderful afternoon and said our goodbyes to head back home. The trip home was uneventful and I arrived in Lawrence just in time for rush hour. I was halfway through town, when something unexpected occurred; as I entered an intersection on a green light, traveling the speed limit of 45 mph., a small silver car turned right on a red light. He hadn't stopped before turning, he just pulled out into my lane at about 10 mph. Directly in back of him was a police vehicle with lights flashing; the police vehicle also came through the red light without first stopping. As I swerved to miss the silver car, the police vehicle turned in to the same lane I was in and almost hit me. I pulled back to the right lane and to the curb to let the officer pass.

The rest of the way home, I was pretty shaky and I was puzzled by the fact that as I replayed the near accident in my mind, I realized that: 1. I didn't have time to think about what to do to avoid hitting the silver car; I just did it; and 2. It was a miracle that in rush hour traffic, I didn't swerve into a car coming up beside me on the left. I realized I didn't have time to look to see if the lane was clear before I swerved, but I also wasn't the least bit concerned about it at the time. About 90 % of the time, I was on that street in rush hour traffic, there was a car to my left. So, I could have hit the silver car, the police officer could have hit me and I could have hit a car on my left; none of these things happened. This incident took place a few days after I had the vision of a fender bender. I had nearly forgotten about the vision because both my granddaughter and grandson had been involved in minor accidents in the week prior to my near miss; I assumed the vision was a warning about one of those accidents. Not only did I receive a warning, but I know my angels were protecting me that day, as they have so many times before.

33

WIND BENEATH MY WINGS

As my journey into increased consciousness continues, I find myself having new and unimaginable experiences. I'm not sure what to call them; I can only describe them at this point.

Recently, I have had multi-sensory visions of myself as a person of about 20 yrs. old, and I am ice skating. I not only see myself I can feel the experience of being on the ice and the breeze my movement creates. I can hear the scritch of the skates as I move across the ice. In these visions, I am remarkably good; good enough to be a professional skater or to compete as an amateur. I am skating alone in a large ice rink and the lights have been dimmed. I skate as though there is music playing, but I can't hear it; I only feel it.

My body feels almost weightless and as I skate, I feel as if I could fly; my movements are graceful and beautiful. I have no fear of falling; I feel my skates in contact with the ice as I move across it. I glide and turn and spin effortlessly. I am not thinking, only experiencing; I feel as if I am creating art. I see no color, all is grayed. I can't see my face, but I know I am the skater and I am lost in the deep pleasure the experience creates inside me.

This vision comes and goes; it is brief and I never see the end of it, as if I am skating forever. In this life, I have never even attempted to ice skate. I did try roller skating a few times and I wasn't very good at it. This vision seems so real to me, that I have to wonder if it's an experience from a previous life, or one I am experiencing simultaneously in another dimension?

The Entwining

A Journey of Transformation

PART SEVEN: DREAM MESSAGES

34

DREAM WEAVER

In my book "Roses and Thorns", I told the story of a recurring dream I had as a young child, it happened in the years before I started going to school. I remember the dream vividly though it has been over 60 yrs. since the last time it came to me.

In the dream, I was asleep in my bed and I woke up and felt compelled to go into my closet and remove one of the concrete stones. The closet was unfinished at the time so the cement blocks were still exposed. I removed a specific block and peered inside the opening. I saw a playground with swings and slides and merry-go-rounds. There were lots of children playing there; I crawled through the opening and joined them. They didn't seem like strangers to me and I felt as if I had been there before. I was normally too shy to join into a situation like that, but I felt quite comfortable in doing so. After what seemed like too short a time, I realized it was time for me to return to my bed. I crawled back through the opening and replaced the block. I got back into my bed and the dream ended.

The dream seemed so real when I woke up that I went into the closet and tried to remove the block; I was disappointed when it wouldn't budge. I really wanted to go back there and I did, but only when the dream returned. The dream made me feel happy and sad at the same time and that was confusing for me. I think most often young children are used to dealing with one emotion at a time.

The dream also seemed to be a catalyst that caused me to begin to think about where I had been before I was born. I never entertained the thought that I hadn't pre-existed somewhere, before being born into my family. I knew I had been somewhere, but I just couldn't remember it and I was puzzled by that.

35

WEDDING BELL BLUES

*A*nother recurring dream I had from an early age, foretold of my future wedding. Somehow, I never doubted that I would someday marry; I never even considered a future alone. I was in no way programmed to think this way; I just knew it would be so. I also knew I would marry at an early age, though I didn't think it would be as young as I was when I actually married.

In my dream, I was in a room that I recognized as being in a church; it was like a dressing room or part of a restroom. I stood looking at myself in a full- length mirror; I was wearing a beautiful white dress, with tiers of lace ruffles down the skirt and I was wearing a long wedding veil.

Then suddenly, I was walking down the aisle of the church toward my bridegroom; he was tall and thin and his hair was dark, but that was all I could see. His face was just blank; as hard as I tried each time I had this dream, I could not identify the person I was marrying. I told myself each time I awoke from this dream, that I would just have to wait until I met the right person.

On my 14th birthday my parents gave me a beautiful cedar chest. It was the first piece of furniture I ever owned and it sits today in my guestroom, filled with all of the things I am too sentimental to get rid of. I immediately began to fill it with things I thought I would need when I established my own home; something I very much looked forward to. There was a small department store in the little town I grew up in and I spent my meager allowance every week, on things to fill my cedar chest.

In the fall of that same year, I started high school and on the morning of the first day, as I was walking into the building, I saw him. I didn't know instantly that this was the person I was going to marry, but I felt this strange shock wave when I first saw him. The groom in my dream could have been described as tall, dark and handsome, but since I never saw his face, I can't say for sure. The guy who walked into the school building at nearly the same moment I did, was tall and had dark hair, very nice white teeth and a dark tan. I didn't think he was handsome, but I thought he was very interesting. Most people either thought he wasn't that great looking, or that his appearance was unusual and they didn't know what to make of him.

I soon found out he was a senior and was new to the school, due to the recent consolidation with some smaller rural schools in our area. Some friends of mine who had already met him, introduced us a couple of weeks later. We dated all through high school; I soon found out he didn't fit in very well with my circle of friends and we had almost no common interests. Nevertheless, I was smitten and soon gave up most of my friends and all of the activities I was involved in, to spend all of my time with him.

At Christmastime of my junior year, he gave me an engagement ring; my parents weren't at all pleased, but they told me I could keep it. I think they thought I'd lose interest and they could avoid a big fight. They did make it clear that I wasn't marrying him, or anyone else until after graduation.

The next summer, we decided to elope; he was 19 and I was sixteen. Our plan was thwarted when he went to the county courthouse to get a license, and the judge thought he was lying about his age. The judge called his parents, who promptly called mine and it erupted into a very ugly scene. I was extremely angry, humiliated and embarrassed. I had the worst fight I ever had with my mother and to my everlasting regret, I actually told her I hated her. If one of my children had ever uttered those words to me, I would have been completely devastated. My father, ever the peacemaker, took it upon himself to break the stalemate my mother and I had reached, and in desperation made a deal with me. I would not run away and stay in school, and he would sign papers for me to get married after my 17th birthday. He knew he was making a deal with the devil, but I'm sure he was desperate and thought it would buy him some time. I'm sure he prayed every day I would change my mind. That almost worked; I went through about a two- week period where I had doubts about what I was doing, but in the end, it didn't last and I went ahead with my plans. In retrospect, I can see heaven was trying to guide me away from making one of the biggest mistakes of my life, in the end, free will won out.

I was a pretty responsible 17 yr. old, but I had failed to consider the fact that other than thinking I was "in love", I had absolutely nothing in common with the person I married. When I later discovered I didn't love him, he turned out to be someone I didn't particularly like either. When it all came crashing down around me, I realized my whole life was a lie, but I tried for five years to live with my mistake; I had, after all, promised God that I would remain faithful to my wedding vows until I died. When it became obvious that I had to get a divorce, I figured God was probably through with me and it became about doing the best thing for my children.

I was determined never to make the same mistake again and promised myself I would never again get married. That was when the person I should have waited for, came into my life; the person God sent to be my husband. It took a lot to convince me to get remarried and I almost didn't accept his proposals; that would have been the greatest mistake of all.

The point I'm trying to make with all of this sordid tale of my personal failings is this: sometimes we just need to hold back and let life come to us. God always has a plan for your life, if you'll just get out of the way and let it unfold. There is a gospel song that says:" stand still and let God move." That's great advice!

There are two aspects of my recurring wedding dream that did come to pass: I was married in a white lace dress with tiers of lace ruffles cascading down the skirt. Amazingly, my mother picked out my dress from a bridal catalog at the dress shop where she worked, without me ever having seen it and I was married in the same church from my dream. The only amusing thing about this whole story, is that at the end of the dream, I discovered the dress was made of toilet paper! That should have told me something!

My wedding gown – nearly identical to the dress in my recurring dream.

36

THE HOUSE YOU LIVE IN

In my book "Roses and Thorns", I wrote about my mother's Aunt Anna, who raised her from the time she was about 3yrs. old and who became in every sense of the word, except biologically, a grandmother to myself and my siblings. This chapter is about Anna also, because her house is a place I have gone to many times in my dreams. Anna's husband Richie, passed away in 1966; she lived to be 80 yrs. old and passed away in 1980. The last few years of her life, I lived in the house I grew up in on Pine Street; it was half a block from Anna's. I moved back home with my two older sons when I was getting a divorce. My parents were moving out of town and I rented the house from them, until Tom and I were married and we bought our first home. I took over responsibility for Anna when my parents moved away. The summer of 1980 was incredibly hot and Anna had no air conditioning in her home. I knew she was suffering from the intense heat and I tried to at least have her sleep at my house, so she would get some relief and could rest. She would get up during the night and go home. Her health was deteriorating and my family and her doctor decided she should go to a nursing home. My mother was in agreement, but could not bring herself to make Anna go if she didn't want to. I didn't want her to die just because it was hot, and I knew she needed basic care that the home could provide.

One day after she had been in the facility a couple of weeks, she told me she hated me for doing that to her. Those words cut me so deeply, but I still believed I had acted out of love and concern for her. A few days later, I was at the public library and the librarian, who was a long-time friend of my mother's said to me; *"You might as well have put a gun to her head and pulled the trigger, because when you take an old person out of their home, they just die!"* I went home and cried for hours. About two weeks before Anna passed away, she told me she was sorry for the things she said to me that day and that she knew I loved her and was just trying to help.

Soon after Anna went to the nursing home, her property was sold to the local school district. The house was demolished and a tennis court and parking lot now stand in its place. I began to have a recurring dream that I was driving in our old neighborhood and I would see Anna's house, and the lights were on inside. I would think: *"Oh my gosh, I haven't checked on her for years!!".* I would stop my car and run inside, calling her name repeatedly. Usually there was no answer and I couldn't find her there. Sometimes, she would be there, but it seemed as if she couldn't hear me and was unaware of my presence. I had many such dreams over about twenty years and then my mother passed in Jan. of 2002. She was raised in Anna's house, so when I saw her in one of my dreams about the house, I asked Mother where she had been since she passed and she replied: *"Oh, I haven't been very far away."*
I remembered that dream and her words to me when she touched my arm 13 yrs. later, shortly before Ethan's life was taken. It was a warning that something shocking was about to happen and I should brace myself for it. I have returned to

Anna's house numerous times in the past 6 yrs. in my dreams, but my mother hasn't been there. Each time the dream repeats itself, I have a hopeful sensation that I'll find her there and she'll speak to me again.

37

DOES ANYBODY REALLY KNOW WHAT TIME IT IS?

This experience is best described as a sudden "knowing" that something has occurred. I haven't received a telepathic communication in the form of a verbal message, and there is no other way to explain how I know. I just do!
I awoke one night quite late, from a sound sleep; I was suddenly and completely wide awake. Almost immediately, I realized I was reliving a memory that involved two couples; the first couple I had been friends with for a few years. The second couple was new in town and I hadn't known them very long. My brief relationship with the second couple didn't end well, and I was very disturbed by the memory that kept repeating itself in my head and would not let me block it. I tried repeatedly to think of something else; some pleasant memory or thought that would get me past the memory I woke up with. This memory was from a time in my life that I try not to revisit and I have asked God's forgiveness for my actions at that time; I know He has forgiven me. Psalm 103:12 says: *"As far as the east is from the west; so far, He has removed our transgressions from us."*

No matter how hard I tried, I couldn't get these thoughts to go away. It was a long time before I could go back to sleep.

When I think of the person I was at that time, it's like thinking about someone else's life. The truth is, I was another person then, and that person was someone I didn't like much.

A couple of days later, I remembered having this experience and mentioned it to my sister; it was still bothering me and I was wondering if something had happened to one of the four people in the memory. The intense experience of this memory took place on Sunday night; on Tuesday night my friend passed.

I believe that any interaction you have with a human spirit creates an entwining. Think of a huge net with a knot that represents each of the interactions between you and another person. These interactions create an entwining in your spirit as well as the spirit you connected with; some of these connections are very brief interactions and some last for eternity.

At about the same time I woke up suddenly thinking about these people from my past, I had begun to see those strange numbers that caught my attention in the months before Ethan passed. In that case, the numbers seemed overwhelmingly ominous; this time it was different. I felt puzzled as to why I was suddenly seeing them again. Many people believe numbers have great significance. The definition of numerology is: any belief in the divine or mystical relationship between a number and one or more coinciding events. In my own experience, I have noticed a number of spiritual events involving the number 3. It was significant in several ways after Ethan's passing; He spoke to me 3 days later, as I was returning to Kansas for his service. It is significant to me that my friend passed three days after I woke up with this very insistent memory of him.

My experiences have taught me not to believe in

coincidence. I say that repeatedly in my writing, because it's usually the first way people try to explain unusual things and I don't think you can say it enough!

38

DEEP IN THE HEART OF TEXAS

As I examine my past, searching for meaning that previously went unnoticed, I realize than often the meaning of our experiences isn't immediately clear; often a lot of time must pass before an experience can be seen in a larger context and begin to reveal its purpose. I do believe everything happens for a reason; sometimes, it's nothing that would seem noteworthy to other people, but in the context of your life, it's the missing piece of information or experience that pulls things together for you. That insignificant event may hold the key to the next step on your personal journey. As an example of what I mean, let me use my encounter with Jesus on the day of Ethan's burial. I instantly recognized it as a significant event, but it was many months before I accepted the fact that the transfiguration I saw that day, was Jesus. I kept trying to find another explanation because I didn't believe that was possible, or likely. When I mentally and emotionally allowed for that possibility, the truth rose in my spirit and was planted in my soul. Truth always brings peace and once I recognized the Truth, it was such a relief. I began to have experiences of spiritual revelation often, and I never doubted the truth again; everything began to have a newfound clarity.

I recently experienced a very unusual dream, at least it seemed like a dream in the beginning. In revisiting the event in a similar way to the encounter with Jesus, I came to realize it was something more than a dream.

Ethan and his family lived in Lubbock, Texas for a number of years. It was where he began his teaching career a few months after receiving his doctorate degree from Kansas University. I was happy that he had received an offer so soon after graduation, but I was a bit sad that it would take him and his family so far away from us. Being that far away from home was a sacrifice for him; he was such a family- oriented person and he loved having both his immediate family and his extended family close by.

Lubbock was over 500 miles from our home in Kansas and I was used to seeing Ethan's family about every 4-6 weeks. I knew I would have to conquer my fear of flying if I was going to get to see them often. Getting to Lubbock by car was a 9 hour drive, more if you actually stopped anywhere and got out of the car. Even on a plane, it was a 9hour day when you count arriving at the airport early, wait time, layover and changing planes etc. When I arrived at the airport, Ethan would pick me up and drive us to the west side of Lubbock, where he and Liz lived in the suburb of Wolfforth. As we drove in from the airport, you would arrive at the same entrance into town that we would come to when we drove. It is an overpass that you go under if you're going through town, or onto the ramp if you take the bypass around Lubbock that is known as the Loop. We always took the north part of the loop and I remember the drive well.

My "dream" began at the overpass that marks the entrance into Lubbock, I knew immediately where I was. I moved up the ramp to the north loop, and onto the highway, but I was not in a vehicle of any kind. My movement was at the normal speed of traffic (about 70 mph). There were vehicles all around me, but I heard no sound. I knew that I didn't have a body; it was just my "being" that was making this journey.

As I traveled, I saw all of the familiar buildings I had seen on my visits to Ethan's family; the football stadium with the new sky boxes, the lights on the field, the red tiled roofs of the mission style buildings on the Texas Tech campus, the Western Heritage Museum where Ethan took me to a wedding gown exhibit, the Ranch and Agricultural Museum, the hospital where my granddaughter was born and the large shopping mall we visited nearly every time I was there. As the Loop swings around to the south, you come to the exit for Wolfforth. I came down off the exit ramp and stopped at the intersection where you would turn right and go over a set of railroad tracks. I noticed the crossing arms were down and the red lights were flashing as if to bar the way. Suddenly the thought entered my mind *"He isn't here."* and the experience ended. I woke up and realized the experience wasn't real.

The hyper-realistic quality of the experience was the first thing that made me question whether it was just a run of the mill dream. The longer I thought about it, I began to see it as more than that. When I thought about the fact that I was traveling at 70 miles per hour, without a body or a vehicle, I knew this was an out of body experience. I don't believe that has ever happened to me before. The only sound I heard during this entire experience was the sound of my own voice, when I realized Ethan wouldn't be there anymore, living in the house he and Liz bought in Wolfforth.

I'm sure I have had other out of body experiences, but I didn't remember them or didn't recognize them for what they truly were.

The Entwining

A Journey of Transformation

PART EIGHT: SPIRITUAL SNAPSHOTS

39

SNAPSHOT

This chapter is a compilation of some very brief spiritual experiences; they happen as quickly as you would snap a photo. They always leave me with a feeling some would refer to as the "warm fuzzies".

DIAMOND GIRL

June 14, 2020, Today I was working in my sewing room; I was pressing some fabric pieces I was going to use to make face masks to donate to the local health clinic. I was listening to Pandora as I was working.

   Just above me on a shelf, was a picture of Ethan and Liz from their wedding; she is wearing the wedding gown I made for her. I remembered the wedding photographer telling me that he and his wife, who was his assistant, had worked about 200 weddings a year for more than 40 years, and they both agreed they had never seen a more beautiful gown.

As I was remembering what the photographer said that day, the song "Diamond Girl" began to play; it is one of the songs Ethan has used in the musical messages he sends me now, to refer to Liz. He was letting me know he was reading my thoughts and he agreed with the photographer's statement about the gown. He told me numerous times at his wedding reception how awesome he thought Liz's dress was, and how beautiful she was in it.

GLORY DAYS

About a week after the Celebration service that honored the life of my brother-in-law Dan, I was again working in my sewing room and listening to music on Pandora. The song "Glory Days", by Bruce Springsteen began to play. When I recognized the song that was playing, I suddenly had chills run up both arms. I immediately thought of Dan, because he had been a big fan of Bruce Springsteen. I knew it was a "hello" from Dan's spirit. I recognize Dan's spirit because I always get that little chill when he's around.

TRACES OF LOVE

One day I was talking to my brother on the phone, as I sat in front of the computer. There is a slide show of pictures that runs continuously on the screen, when it is not in use. Ethan put all of the pictures on it 7 or 8 years ago. Most of them are pictures he took, or is in. My brother didn't know about the pictures that were running on my screen as we talked. Out of the blue, he mentioned a picture that would occasionally come up on its own on his computer. It was a picture of Ethan and his oldest son Connor, taken on the day Ethan received his PhD. and Connor graduated from Hilltop preschool, also affiliated with the University of Kansas. They are both wearing blue graduation caps and gowns. They walked in the procession down the hill into the football stadium together on that day; a longstanding tradition at KU graduation exercises. No sooner had my brother mentioned the picture, than it appeared on my screen. It was a message from Ethan that he was listening to our conversation and remembering the day also.

FLY AWAY

Another day, I was sitting in my yard swing, talking to my daughter-in-law Carol, on the phone. Our school mascot is the cardinal; they are pretty plentiful here and we see them often, but once in a while we see one acting a bit strangely and we have learned to pay close attention. The yard swing is in a part of our yard that we have been working hard to turn into a private garden sanctuary; we love spending time there.

Carol and I were talking about a text message I received from the mother of the man who took Ethan's life. It was in response to a letter I sent her a couple of weeks prior. As we talked, a cardinal landed on the fountain, a few feet in front of the swing; it stayed there for a couple of minutes, in spite of the fact I was sitting only a few feet away and I was also talking and the swing was creaking. Birds who land there usually fly away immediately when they realize someone is close by. After the cardinal sat on the fountain, it flew to a nearby chair and perched there for an extended period; it then flew into the lattice on the pergola, turned to look at me, and flew off. Altogether, it was an unusually lengthy visit and not the first time Ethan's spirit has visited in the form of a cardinal.

IN THE GARDEN

We usually see more cardinals in early spring and during

the winter months. We nearly always see them in bunches when it snows. The sight of that bright red plumage against the backdrop of crystal white snow is breathtaking. One day this past winter, Tom and I went out to go for a drive in the countryside. As I got in his car, I reached down to put my purse on the floor and when I looked up, I saw in the bare branches of the mulberry tree in the garden, there were seven bright red cardinals. I was surprised to see so many at once and especially on the side of the house away from the feeders. I have learned to pay attention to things that appear out of the ordinary; someone may be trying to tell me something.

THE MESSENGER

My husband recently had some lab tests done to determine why he wasn't feeling his usual energetic self. We were told not to expect the results for a week. Waiting for test results from a doctor is always a bit nerve-wracking; your imagination can run wild.

The day after the tests were completed, I left my house to run an errand. As I got in my car, I inadvertently looked up at the sky; flying way up high, directly over my house, was a large eagle. I was thrilled, I love eagles and I get really excited when I see one. My first thought was: *"Eagles are messengers!"* That afternoon, the Dr's. office called with the results of Tom's tests; six days early! The key to receiving messages of this kind is to keep an open mind and pay attention!

WHERE HAVE YOU GONE

Yesterday, as I sat at the island in my kitchen eating my lunch, Ethan's spirit dropped in spontaneously and expressed his appreciation for something Tom and I had done for his family, earlier that day. I went from absentmindedly eating my lunch, to being moved to tears by the sudden and unexpected sound of his voice. When he communicates something that way, the same way he did just 3 days after his passing, it is so reaffirming of what I know and what so many others believe is impossible, that it makes me burst into tears. I can't prove that any of the things I've written about in this book are real or true, but I know they are in a way that causes me to have no more doubt about them than the fact that I live and breathe.

When I say my new life is very similar to my old life, I'm talking about my spirit life; my physical life has changed drastically in the past 6 yrs. Ethan is always within my reach in a spiritual sense; as with all parents who live their lives without the physical presence of their child, I miss him every minute of every day. The gift of having him with me in spirit is indescribably comforting and I wish with all my heart I could share it with everyone else who loves and misses him.

WILDWOOD FLOWER

My oldest son Brett, often tells me he can detect the strong odor of hairspray, when he is alone driving in his car. He specifically says it smells like my mother's hairspray: AquaNet.

My mother was very short and she always did what she could to make herself look taller. She felt like people had a tendency to not take you seriously if you were short. She wore spike heels and a bouffant hairstyle that required huge amounts of hairspray to maintain. She used AquaNet for many years; her grandchildren fondly recall her having so many empty hairspray cans, that they could use them like bowling pins, along with the tennis ball they found in her toy box.

Mother's hair was difficult to style and as she got older and it became much thinner, it required even more hairspray. My sister, Jeanne, inherited our paternal grandmother's beautiful thick hair, easy to manage and grow quite long; I got Mother's difficult hair. Mom's hair was much darker than any of her children's, but mine gets darker right before turning silver. I also use a lot of hairspray, but not AquaNet. I wonder if that will be the way my children and grandchildren recognize my spirit, when I'm gone; by the scent of my hairspray. I'm sure Mother doesn't mind being remembered that way; I know she just wants to be remembered fondly and so she is, and much more often than she would have believed.

BORN IN THE USA

This morning as I sat down at the island in my kitchen to have a bowl of cereal with bananas, I looked at a picture of my brother-in-law Dan, it's on the memorial program from Dan's Celebration of Life service, that is still on my refrigerator door. Dan passed in March of 2020, but I feel his spirit close by every now and then. As I looked at Dan's picture, I said to him *"Oh Dan, you lived a good life; you were successful at doing the thing you loved to do."* Then I heard him reply: *"I like bananas, you know."* I said: *"Yes I know that. I made some bread and butter pickles. I wish I could give you some."* Then he said: *"That's okay, I can taste them."* I said: *"You can?" "Yes,"* he said. Then I asked him: *"What are you doing?"* He said: *"I'm directing."* I said: *"That's great!"* Then he said: *"You can be successful too, just keep writing; I think you should do the mediumship thing you are considering. "You do?* I said; *"Yes, I do!"* At this point, Dan's presence receded and I sensed my husband's Grandmother Mininger was present; she said: *"We've got our eye on Dan, we'll take care of Dan; you take care of Tom!" I said: I can do that."*

After I finished my breakfast, I went outside to check my car; it sometimes gets water in the floorboards, when it rains really hard and we had experienced a thunderstorm during the night. I opened the driver's side door and turned the key to open the windows and let some fresh air in, as I did that, the radio came on; it was playing "Born in the USA", by Bruce Springsteen. Dan loves Bruce Springsteen! It was confirmation that the conversation I just had was real and not imagined.

Ethan and Conner at KU graduation – a big day for them both.

The Entwining

A Journey of Transformation

PART NINE:
ANIMAL SPIRITS

40

BUTTERFLY KISSES

On the day before Ethan's celebration service, we had a large number of people at our house; most were family or close friends. There were several children there and at one point Jeff and Carol decided they needed to get them out for some fresh air and a break from the heaviness of the atmosphere in the house. They decided to take them to the city park; they all walked there together. The park is about ten blocks from the house we were living in. As they were enjoying the park, a sudden heat shower came up and sent them all running for cover in the shelter house. The rain shower was over in a few minutes and they decided to walk back home. They noticed immediately after the rain that the sky above them was teeming with monarch butterflies. That wouldn't have been unusual in itself, because they come through our area every year on their migration to Mexico. The interesting thing was that the butterflies followed them home; they stayed overhead for the full ten blocks and hung around over their heads long enough for Carol to come inside to get me, so I could see them. There were at least a dozen butterflies circling over my granddaughter Taylor's head, when I got outside.

Since that day, monarchs have become something spiritual

in our world; we often go to monarch launch activities in our area. The monarchs have been resting in protective net enclosures where they lay eggs and recover from their travel. We are able to hold them in our hands after they are tagged with a small adhesive sticker, and then they launch themselves into the air to begin the next stretch of their migration journey.

I have begun to include flowers and shrubs in my flower garden that are butterfly friendly. The monarchs are becoming endangered because of the loss of such plants due to the use of pesticides and destruction of their habitat areas. I was sad to notice we had so few butterflies this year and I hope they will return in greater numbers next season.

Butterflies just make me happy and joyful; I have no idea why that is, but I suspect there are spirits nearby when I see them. I sometimes see pairs of large yellow butterflies and my parents come to mind instantly. I have discovered butterflies can be used to symbolize many different things and can deliver a variety of messages.

41

WINGS OF A DOVE

In April of 2016, seven months after losing my son, I flew to Washington D.C. with my sister Jeanne, to visit her daughter. It had taken that long for me to recover some semblance of balance and regain my physical strength enough to make the trip. It was my second time to experience D.C. and on my first trip I discovered it was a place I very much enjoyed visiting; this trip was to fulfill a promise I made to my niece, Leyla.

Leyla and Ethan grew up together, attended the same high school and were in many of the same activities. They were more like brother and sister than cousins. She was nearly inconsolable when she received the news that Ethan's life had been taken. She was also upset that it wasn't possible for her to come home to be with our family and to attend the Celebration of Life service for Ethan. She was about 3 weeks away from giving birth to her second son and her doctor advised against making the trip.

As our plane was landing at National Airport in D.C. on that beautiful April day, I saw a building in the distance that I didn't recognize; Jeanne said it was the National Cathedral. I felt drawn to it and knew I needed to go there. When Leyla asked if there were any sites I particularly would like to visit, it was the only thing on my list.

The cathedral itself was beautiful, but I knew that wasn't why I felt guidance to go there. It was emotional to stand in the main sanctuary and recognize it from the numerous solemn occasions I've witnessed there on TV. The stained glass in the windows, high above the marble floors, are magnificent blues, reds, golds and greens. I have always loved Gothic architecture and everything about the building was breathtaking.

We made our way down to the crypt below the main sanctuary and in the smaller "Bethlehem Chapel", we attended a Communion service. I felt my emotions rising as I listened to the words of the presiding Bishop and took the sacraments. It was the first time I had taken Communion in over a decade.

The visiting officiant that day was a woman; I didn't catch her name, but the nametag she wore said she was from Salt Lake City. I wish I had paid attention to her name, because I would like to tell her how her words that day changed my life. As she began to speak, I knew this was why I needed to go there; I found my reason to go on living and to live with new purpose. The words she spoke that day were as if God was speaking directly to me; I'm sure she has been used that way many times before in her service to the church, but I wonder if she is aware of it when it occurs.

When we returned home from our trip, several days later, there was a beautiful surprise waiting for me. I was in the back seat of my brother-in-law's car when he pulled into my driveway and I heard him say: *"What the heck is that doing there?"* By the time I had released my seatbelt and leaned forward to see what it was, I nearly missed it; a beautiful male ringneck pheasant. It was standing in my driveway, in the middle of town, at the moment I returned home from a trip that changed my life forever. The colors of the pheasant were the same brilliant reds, blues, golds and greens of the stained glass in the cathedral. Pheasants are plentiful in Kansas and seeing one is common, but I have never before seen one in the middle of town, standing in my driveway; not ever! I recognized it instantly, as a message from Ethan; I had felt him with us each place we went in D.C. He visited there often and because of his love of history, it held special significance to him.

42

RUN FOR THE ROSES

I believe spirit is active all around us, at all times; we are just mostly unaware of it. We chalk it up to imagination, coincidence or mistaken perceptions. It would be easy to think that the spiritual activity around me began after Ethan passed, but the reality is that my perception of spirit is what changed. There is spirit in every living thing; that includes animals, plants, trees; basically, all of nature. I have had some unusual experiences with animals such as birds, squirrels and most particularly a horse. I related this story in an earlier book and include it here because it was a supernatural occurrence.

I would never refer to myself as a true animal lover, that description would more closely fit my sister, Jeanne. I have always admired animals, but usually from a distance; that is particularly true of large dogs and horses. I think horses are amazingly beautiful and magnificent creatures, but I am intimidated by their size. Jeanne has been in love with them since she was about three years old. She has a healthy respect for them, but no fear.

About a year after Ethan passed, Jeanne and I visited our cousins in Arkansas. They live in a beautiful secluded valley about an hour from Fayetteville. We spent three incredibly relaxing days there in the serenity and peace of the valley.

They have a variety of animals they share their lives with; Jeanne was instantly drawn to the horses. My cousin acquired a young horse that was being groomed for a racing career. Sadly, he developed a weakness in one of his legs and had to be retired after only a few times out.

Jeanne and I went to meet him the morning after we arrived and as I stood at a safe distance, she stood next to the fence and fed him apples, while they had a non-verbal conversation. My cousin calls him "Red", but I call him "King". That's not his full name, but I think it suits him, because he is a particularly majestic specimen; the picture of strength and endurance.

We went out to say goodbye to the horses on the morning we left the valley to return home. Jeanne fed him more apples and I stood in my same spot admiring him. At one point, he seemed to be looking directly into my eyes; it was as if he too, was saying goodbye. I was fascinated by him and thought he was one of the most beautiful animals I'd ever seen, but that was all, or so I thought.

The morning after we arrived home, I was enjoying my morning coffee and thinking that the trip had been just what I needed. I wasn't really thinking about King that morning, but strangely, I felt his indomitable spirit reach across the hundreds of miles between us and speak to my heart. It was as if he was offering me his strength and courage, which at that time, when I was still deep in grief I needed badly. In that moment, I felt something I can only describe as a "ZING" and I was suddenly head over heels about that horse. For weeks I showed his picture to everyone I talked to; that was so totally out of character for me, even I couldn't believe I did it.

We visited our cousins again the following year and I was as anxious to see King as to see my family members. We stopped at a grocery store in Fayetteville and I picked up flowers for our hostess and apples for King. I think of him often and I am grateful to his spirit, he inspires me. He was just one of many animals who revealed their spirits to me during my grief, and as I have walked the long road of recovery.

King of Hearts – This very special creature reached across hundreds of miles to share his strength and courage with me.

43

THE EAGLE AND THE HAWK

I am a bird-lover, I'm fascinated with their incredible variety of color and song. I am astonished at their ability to navigate, migrate and find suitable places to inhabit. There are about ten-thousand bird species; I do have my favorites, among them are cardinals and red-tail hawks, but by far the object of my greatest fascination is the eagle. I went many years without seeing an eagle in the wild, but since Ethan's passing, I have seen about a dozen or so.

One day my husband and I were driving past the Baker wetlands at Lawrence, Ks. I was looking out over the shallow pond for birds and noticed two eagles about 20 ft. apart, each was sitting in a tree, looking over the pond and toward the road; their heads followed the movement of our car as we passed by them.

Within a minute of seeing them, I thought of my father; he used to be a pretty good guitarist and he liked playing instrumentals. One of his favorites was called: Under The Double Eagle, that thought made seeing the two eagles sitting side by side, especially significant for me.

In my first book, I wrote about a red-tail hawk who came to visit my front yard one day. About a week before he made his appearance, I was going for a drive in the country and saw a large hawk sitting atop a pole. As I drove past him, I said to myself, but meant for him: *"Mr. Hawk, why don't you come hang out in my yard, so I can see you every day?"* As Tom and I arrived home from a grocery shopping trip, there stood a large red-tail hawk in our yard under the bird feeder. I live in town and though hawks sometimes fly over the town, it is pretty unusual for them to be seen on the ground, close to where people are. The hawk was feeding on a small bird, who was unlucky enough to catch it's attention and become his lunch.

    I was able to walk within 3 or 4ft. of him and he didn't seem to be bothered by my presence. He stayed on the ground for about five more minutes, before flying away; I was able to take several pictures of him.

    Before my son passed, I rarely took notice of hawks; they are not particularly pretty birds and though they have a dignity of spirit, they are not as majestic as eagles. I began to notice some unusual behavior when I saw them and the more I paid attention to them, the more easily I could recognize the spirit within them. As your own spiritual senses are awakened, you begin to see spirit all around you. One of the most surprising things I saw, was when I realized there was spirit in falling snow. I believe there is spirit in all living things and I had to think a bit to understand how there could be spirit in snowflakes. Snow is frozen water and if you've ever looked at a droplet of water under a microscope, you realize it is very much alive. I have never looked at snow the same way since that day. There is truly much more to this world than meets the eye, or the five senses.

The hawk who came to visit one afternoon.

44

FOREVER AUTUMN

September is always a difficult month for me and I try to get through it the best way I can. Ethan's life was taken on September 14, 2015. His birthday is about 2 weeks following that day, on the 27th. It's a little easier to get through that day, because it's a day to celebrate his coming into our lives. I made it through pretty well this year until evening fell and with it, I had a recurring thought running through my mind: *"This is the day we got our baby."* That used to be a happy thought, but our "baby" isn't here with us now and we miss him terribly.

I am fortunate that I can feel his presence and hear his voice every day of my life, but it seems most of my other family members can't and sometimes I feel guilty about that.

This year before we made it through Ethan's birthday, my last living aunt passed away. She was 91 years old and the last of my father's family, that included his parents and 8 siblings. Now they and all of their spouses have left this world and for us it is the passing of a generation; it makes me sad. This is the curse of a large family; you bury a lot of people that you care about.

Within 10 days of my aunt's burial, we learned another family member had passed unexpectedly; his name was Jeremy, and he was only about 50 years old. There have been other times in my life when it seemed as if the dominos were falling too fast. It becomes really hard to maintain your balance in those times, and now we are all trying to maintain constant vigilance against Covid-19. All in all, it weighs heavily.

I am nearly a recluse these days and for the most part I prefer it that way, but when I need some fresh air and sunshine, or a change of scenery, I get in the car and drive out through the countryside; even a 20 or 30 minute drive out in nature seems so refreshing to my spirit.

Yesterday, when I went for my morning drive, I saw what at first looked like two large turkey buzzards flying together, but then I saw a flash of white on the tail of one of the birds and I realized it could be an eagle. I watched as it climbed higher in the sky and I could see its whole body; it was an eagle and I was thrilled! I watched until it was out of my sight and then continued on to my destination. I picked up some lunch and had intended to return home down another road. Instead, I decided to go back down to the road where I had seen the eagle and try to spot it again.

When I arrived at nearly the same location where I first saw the eagle, a large bird flew from the south into the opposite ditch and landed there. I had slowed down to a crawl because there was no other traffic; I was hoping the bird would stay on the ground, so I could get a real good look at him. Instead, just as I got to where he was, the eagle flew back across the road, directly in front of my car at about eye level. He was magnificent and I was so thrilled, I was literally giggling and clapping my hands like a 5 yr. old. Seeing him immediately lifted my mood and I drove home happily.

Today, I decided to return to where I had seen the eagle the day before. This time there was no sign of him, but I had a surprise there anyway. As I approached the place where the eagle had been the day before, my Pandora station suddenly stopped playing the song I was listening to and began playing "Pachelbel's Canon in D"; Ethan's "goodnight song". I hear it nearly every night before I go to sleep. As soon as the song ended, my station went right back to playing the country pop and rock I had been listening to. Pachelbel's Canon is classical music, written about 1680; it definitely didn't belong on that station. I have never had Pandora stop in the middle of any song, unless I wanted to move on to something else and pressed the appropriate button.

   This tells me Ethan had a hand in the eagle sighting from the day before. He sends me these kinds of gifts frequently and they always take my breath away. I see them because I am receptive to seeing them and I know better than to talk myself out of my first impressions of what they are and where they come from. As soon as you open your heart and mind to these spiritual gifts, they begin to occur more and more often. This is why I wrote this book, so you would see that there is more to life than we believe there is.

The Entwining

PART TEN: GUIDANCE

45

WHERE HE LEADS ME

I have discovered through my own experiences that spiritual revelation usually comes in bits and pieces, and not necessarily in an easily recognized form. It isn't like a book or movie, for instance, it generally doesn't come with a discernable beginning, middle and ending. Often the first bit of information that comes means little to you until the next revelation, or the one after that gradually puts it all into the right order. This is why it's so important when seeking spiritual guidance, not to dismiss anything as coincidence or irrelevant. You just store it away until you receive that piece of the puzzle that makes it all fall into place. You may ask yourself, *"Why does it seem as if spirit is playing games with me? Can't they just say what they mean?"* I'm not positively sure why they don't, but I suspect it happens the way it does because we often aren't ready to handle the full unvarnished truth and they are trying to prepare us. If we aren't spiritually mature enough to have all of the answers, they don't give them to us. Sometimes, only knowing part of the answer creates a desire to know more and encourages us to seek the rest of the story. The more time we spend focused on the spiritual world, the easier it becomes to recognize the guidance that is being given to us.

Many of the things I've written about in this book, happened before Ethan's life was taken. It was only after that cataclysmic event altered my life and my trajectory, that I began to seek deeper knowledge of spirit realms. I have found that my heart will tell me when I've got the real message I'm being sent. If I feel off balance and my peace is disturbed in some way, I know I'm not there yet and I need to keep trying to interpret what I'm receiving.

Many times, the most obvious answer isn't the right answer; there have been a couple of occasions where I went with the obvious interpretation, only to discover that a non-related occurrence had masked the real message. It's kind of like the thing writer's do in mystery novels by throwing in some seemingly important, but totally irrelevant information to see if they can fool you into believing it's part of the information needed to solve the mystery. It's called a "red herring".

Many people mistakenly believe that heavenly guidance is just meant to help you when you return to the spiritual realm; they couldn't be more mistaken. We all walk in the world of humans and the world of spirit simultaneously and much of what happens here is to foster growth that impacts us in the here and now, as well as in the hereafter. The universe is constantly sending us messages; think of them as rays of sunlight. They are meant to "en-lighten" us.

46

THE LIVING YEARS

A few days ago, my husband and I invited his mother to our home for a cookout. She lives about 20 miles away and my husband goes there to take her to get her groceries and for doctor's appointments; so, she doesn't often come here.

We had a nice lunch and then the three of us spent several hours catching up on family news etc. We all moved to this area few years ago, from the same small town, so we spent some time sharing any news we had of our mutual acquaintances who still live there.

Out of the blue, Nellie, (my mother-in-law) asked me about a longtime friend of mine. She said: *"I notice you haven't mentioned her lately? Are you no longer friends?"* I explained that I had been in a quandary about my relationship with the friend, because we have grown apart in many ways. My friend has been very good to me and has done a lot of nice things, especially after Ethan's passing. I don't want to hurt her or make her feel abandoned, but I feel my guidance is telling me I need to let go.

I often get a little buzz of energy before I receive messages from my spirit guides; a burst of energy like a "zing". The next words out of Nellie's mouth came straight from my guides, through her, to me: *"I'm sure you've done a lot of nice things for her too, but sometimes you just have to call it even and move on."* This was not the first time I received this message, but the others weren't so direct, or obvious. I'm sure Nellie had no idea how impactful those words would be when she uttered them. I have learned to recognize these times when spirit uses someone to deliver a message like this. When you are the person heaven chooses to deliver a very direct message, you will probably not be aware of what has just happened. I was looking to have the previous thoughts I was assuming to be spiritual messages affirmed, and there it was.

    The message is to let go, however, there has been no guidance as to how to do that. I'm afraid that part will have to come from me. Letting go has always been hard for me; I become attached to people, places and things easily. I have come to know in my heart that letting go is one of the things I came here to learn; I'm working on it.

47

WHAT'S YOUR NAME?

As my spiritual journey has progressed, I've reached a point where the road has forked once again; one path takes me to a place I can't begin to see now and the other is leading me to study mediumship. As usual, my sense of practicality asks me: *"What would you do with such knowledge?"* My answer at this point is: *"At the least, it might help me with my writing; at the utmost it could lead me to become a practicing medium."* As with any such question that arises, I have sought guidance from more than one source. I haven't received all of the answers yet, but then, it doesn't come in the blink of an eye. When I get impatient for answers, I often hear a voice say *"wait for it!"*

I recently ordered a set of audio CDs, that are designed to assist in training you for mediumship and I also ordered several books authored by the same woman, who has been a practicing medium for over a decade. I try to order used books whenever necessary because I read a lot and it runs into a lot of money; especially if I only read the book once and then get rid of it. When the books arrived, I selected the one I wanted to read first; I opened to the title page and discovered it had been signed by the author. The inscription read *"To Jeff, with love and thanks!"*; that was followed by the signature. What made this significant to me, is that my first name is Jeffery. Now I realize the inscription wasn't meant for me, but it is significant that out of all the used copies of this book for sale online, I chose one with an inscription that was addressed to someone of the same name. What could the odds in favor of that be?? I see this "coincidence" as a sign I should examine mediumship deeply enough to make an informed decision about whether it should be part of my journey going forward. It remains to be seen what my next step will be, or where it will take me; that keeps the journey exciting!

48

A LIVING PRAYER

Today is October 23, it is a cold, damp and windy day and the sky has been a pale shade of gray all day; it feels very much like winter. I have spent most of the day in the cozy warmth of my home; my beautiful little Victorian cottage.

I put clean sheets on my very comfy bed, that adjusts with the touch of a button to a position that relieves my chronic back pain. When it came time to prepare our evening meal, my husband and I had many options as to what to eat. After our meal we had leftovers to put in our refrigerator. When I finished in the kitchen, I put on pajamas and sat down in my comfy, plush recliner. I turned on my heating pad which also relieves my back pain and drew a blanket over my lap and feet to keep them warm. Later, when I go to bed, I will turn out the lights and check the locks on the doors; I will feel safe and secure as I drift off to sleep.

Today as I have done all of these things, thoughts come back to me of a homeless man to whom I handed a small amount of cash, earlier this week, as he sat by the drive thru lane of a popular fast-food restaurant, shivering in the damp cold wind. As I handed him the small amount of money through my car window, his eyes met mine, blue eyes just like my son

Jeff's. In fact, nearly everything about him looked like Jeff; the height, the build, the beard, even his voice was similar. At that moment, as I looked into his eyes, I saw uncertainty, embarrassment and loss. I heard a voice in my head say to me *"This is someone's child!"* and that realization broke my heart. For days now, whenever I think of him, I burst into tears. My heart aches for him and for all those who love him. I don't know how or why he ended up living on the street and it doesn't matter to me; he asked for my help and I gave it.

Through this young man, God revealed to me the love and compassion He has for each of His children and that we are supposed to have for each other. It was such a profound experience and though I have always had compassion for the homeless, my desire to help them in whatever way I can, has been substantially deepened and I am changed by it.

The Entwining

A Journey of Transformation

PART ELEVEN: REVELATIONS

49

COAT OF MANY COLORS

My heart has always been captured by things that make me feel sentimental or nostalgic; I never knew why that was until recently. It is so hard for me to part with anything that was given to me by someone I love, or something that was passed down to me by a relative or friend. I am even sentimental in my relationship to the houses I have lived in and the cars I have owned. I save most of the greeting cards I receive; my husband has a particular talent for selecting beautiful cards. I have amassed a forty-seven-year collection of the beautiful Valentines, birthday, anniversary and Mother's Day cards he's given me. My cedar chest is filled to overflowing with these and other treasures, such as, photographs, baby clothes and baby shoes etc. I know that most of these things are meaningless to nearly everyone else, but I still treasure them.

Recently, I started photographing all of the most important family things; so that at least, when my children sort through them after I'm gone, they will know what they are throwing away.

In January of 2021, my mother will have been gone from the physical world for 18 yrs.; every year since then, before the holidays, I put the Christmas quilt she made on the bed in my guestroom. My mother was a seamstress for many years, but she was relatively new to quilting at the time she passed; I believe she had only finished about four quilts. The quilt I have is called "Twelve Days of Christmas". Each appliqued block represents one element of the song it is named for (a partridge in a pear tree, for example). There are hundreds of tiny pieces that Mother machine appliqued to the blocks; a difficult and time-consuming process if you did it by hand, but even harder on the sewing machine. It must have taken her a very long time to complete the twelve blocks, then assemble the quilt top and hand quilt it as she held it on her lap. The quilt isn't actually finished; the basting stitches she put in it when she last worked on it, are still there. I gave some thought to finishing it myself, but thought better of it. Something about seeing the place where she stopped, makes me feel a stronger connection to her. It will never be finished; just as her life will never be finished. She is still living; just in another dimension.

It isn't what I would call a beautiful piece of work, but I still love it. I thought I loved it because it was something Mother made and was proud of. This year was different; I put the quilt on the bed and a couple of weeks later I had one of those spiritual surprises that always warms my heart.

I love Christmas and my mother did too. I love Christmas trees and I usually decorate at least a couple of large ones and several smaller trees as well. I also have a large English Christmas village. Every evening before I go to bed, I walk through and turn off all of the Christmas lights and the table lamps; I call it "putting my house to bed". There is a small tree on the cedar chest, in the guest room where Mother's quilt is. One night I went in to turn off the lights and I absentmindedly ran my hand across the quilt; I suddenly felt my mother's spirit in the room. I stood at the foot of the four-poster bed and leaned over onto the quilt; I put my face down on it and ran my hands over it again. In that moment, I realized that the essence of her spirit is actually in the quilt, just as there is spirit in all things that make us nostalgic. What a beautiful Christmas gift that was!

Forensic scientists tell us we leave our DNA (our personal genetic code) all over the place, on everything we touch, everywhere we go. The experience I had with Mother's quilt tells me we leave a bit of our spirit the same way. So, in fact, our loved ones haven't truly left us, at least not entirely. There is something of them still here with us, we just have to feel it with our spiritual senses and recognize it for what it is.

My mother's Christmas quilt.

50

JUST AS I AM

This morning as I prayed, I received this revelation: My cousin Marty had recently passed, and as I prayed, I asked that his spirit be blessed; it was then that I received this teaching. *We all come exactly as we are at the moment we transition from the world of time, to the world of eternity. We each retain our free will and have the option of growing spiritually to higher levels of transcendence or we can choose to remain at the spiritual level with which we entered into eternity. There is no judgement, if we choose to remain as we are; there is only acceptance and love.*

My cousin lived a pretty solitary life and I wonder if that's really what he wanted or just what his circumstances dictated? He was the last surviving member of his immediate family. He had cared for his mother in her latter years, but she passed a number of years ago. His only sibling, a brother, also passed years ago. His brother had divorced the mother of his children and they were not raised to be close to their father's family. That left Marty with a few fishing buddies that he spent time with. We don't know the circumstances of Marty's passing; I would assume he was alone when the time came for him to go. I prayed he wasn't feeling any fear or sadness at being alone at the end of his life here.

As a spiritual person, and follower of Jesus, I know we are never really alone. Jesus said in Matthew 28:20, *"I am with you always, even to the end of the earth"*. He is there even when we are unaware of His presence.

At this time, we know almost nothing of Marty's passing or the handling of his remains; only that he was cremated and the ashes were claimed, but we don't know who it was that they were released to .We don't know if they were buried or scattered or if they sit in a closet somewhere. We don't know where, or if, there will ever be a stone that bears his name and records that he lived a life here. All of these unknowns are disturbing to me; it feels as if he just vanished without a trace.

51

ALL I NEED IS A MIRACLE

My sister is fascinated with genealogy and recently she discovered an old newspaper article relating to our maternal grandfather. I've written about him in another book and until recently we knew very little about him.

The article Jeanne found, relates a chilling story that reveals the fact that my whole life has been a miracle; it very nearly didn't happen at all. My grandfather was accidentally shot in the abdomen when he was around 20 years old. The contents of the shotgun shell traveled upward at an angle through his body and caused near fatal injuries. He was about 20 miles from a hospital and could easily have bled to death. His survival from such devastating injuries is nothing short of a miracle. He went on to marry my grandmother and father two children, one of whom was my mother; that is also a miracle.

My mother was tiny all of her life; she was born weighing only 3 lbs. There were no neonatal units or pediatric ICU's in those days (1929) and her survival at that weight is also a miracle. Later in her life she had chronic back problems and was told she had been born with spina bifida, which had repaired itself on its own; another miracle. My mother gave birth to 4 children, most likely another miracle. I have come to the conclusion I was meant to be born and in spite of all of these things, I was born a very healthy child and have enjoyed good health up to this point. I can see God's hand in my life even before I was born. I see God's patience as He waited all these years for me to become the person I was destined to be. I have a purpose; something unknown to me as of yet, but I feel myself closing in on it. I believe it will come about through my writing; though it probably hasn't come yet. Writing seems as natural as breathing to me and I hope to be able to continue doing it as long as I live in this world. Whatever this thing is that I am destined to do, may not change the trajectory of the world; in fact, it may only impact one person, but that doesn't make it a mission of less importance. We all are destined to change the world in some way or other and most of us will never recognize what it was that we did, or said, or created, that had an impact, but it doesn't matter. For each of us the gift is in the doing, in the creating and in the giving. Don't let the opportunity to take part in a miracle pass you by unnoticed.

A Journey of Transformation

The Entwining

PART TWELVE: REFLECTIONS

52

FUNNY HOW TIME SLIPS AWAY

When I was a young child, about elementary school age, I couldn't wait for summer vacation. I never liked school and I longed to have the freedom I enjoyed before I started to kindergarten. As a matter of fact, I think my dislike of school goes back even farther than my horrible first day of kindergarten. My brother is a little less than two years older than me and the year he went to school was one of the loneliest times of my life. He was my primary playmate and it was his sense of adventure and imagination that fueled our fun-filled days together. I was so lost without him, that I can't remember having any fun at all until summer vacation arrived, and he was free to spend all day with me again until the school bell rang in early September.

As kids, we were outside all day, every day; we went out right after breakfast and only went home when we got hungry to have lunch. After lunch we were back out till Mother called us in for supper, after which we stayed out till the stars were twinkling overhead.

When you are a small child, you have no idea how it feels to have your life dissected by schedules and bells, and buzzers. It always felt like punishment to me to have to go every day and be told what to think about, and when; I guess I have always had an undisciplined mind. I felt like my mind was the one thing that truly belonged to me. I believed my mind was for creating, and math and science just didn't spark my creativity. My teachers always accused me of daydreaming, but I was either creating something in my mind, or thinking deep thoughts about who I was and how I got here.

It seemed to me that my imprisonment would never end. I couldn't wait to graduate from high school; as it turned out, I had enough credits to graduate after the first semester of my senior year, so at least I was able to cut it short by a few months. I had no real plans once I was free, but I just knew it would be great.

Not too surprisingly, the first few years weren't all that great; I married young, got a divorce, and got remarried. It was at that point things finally began to fall into place; but the metamorphosis continues to this day. It has picked up tremendous speed in the six years since my son has been here in spirit only.

At some point I discovered that it wasn't learning that I didn't like, it was having to learn things I didn't think were relevant. Some of the things I rejected have turned out to be quite relevant; take geometry for instance, when I learned to quilt, I wished I had paid more attention.

I have spent a great many years, trying to educate myself about a lot of things that I felt were important or necessary to being a good wife, mother and friend.

When I began to raise my children, I felt as if the life I had then, which I loved, would go on forever; that period of my life actually lasted about 20 years. You never stop being a parent, but your role suddenly shifts from being the director, to being more of a consultant. Suddenly, you seem to have a lot of time on your hands and you realize you get to determine how you will spend those "extra" hours. The truth is, there are no "extra" hours, just as there is no "extra" money.

While my children were still at home, I worked at various things to make "extra" money. Or I guess, a more accurate statement would be that I made money that allowed us to afford some of the "extra" things our children needed or wanted. I did whatever I could that would allow me to be at home when the kids were home. Only once in my entire life, have I had a full-time job. The job itself was interesting, but as with school, it felt a lot like prison; I didn't keep that job very long.

A few years after Ethan went to college, my first grandchild was born and I realized another phase of my life was beginning. I love being a grandmother and I can't believe how fast my grandchildren have grown up; the youngest turned 11 this year.

The reason for focusing on all of this is that as I look back on my life, I see that some very distinctive lines can be drawn between each phase. This, in spite of the fact that I spent so much time resisting things that I felt compartmentalized my life.

I recently read a book by Mitch Albom, who is one of my favorite authors, the book is titled "The Timekeeper". It is about a fictional character who invented time and was held prisoner because of his invention. The point of the story is that the more you divide time into segments, the faster life flies past. In the end, when the timekeeper finds himself needing just a few more seconds of time (life)to make something come out right, his time has run out and he is abandoned by his own creation.

Each of us is only given a set amount of time here and no

one knows when the hour glass will be empty. When you reach a point in life where it becomes obvious that you likely have more time behind you than ahead, each moment becomes that much more precious. You wish you had savored all of the best moments so much more, because you can never get them back. Time is relentless; it only moves in one direction. In the Harry Potter books, there is a magical device called a "time turner"; it allows the possessor to turn back time to a certain point, so they can change something that has already occurred.

How many times have I wished I could turn time back to the minutes before the tragedy that took Ethan's life occurred; just that much time with the knowledge I have now, might allow that instant to play out another way. Perhaps, I would call him and tell him to leave his office sooner or perhaps, if I had called him at home that morning, he wouldn't have been in his office on campus. This is all wishful thinking and so pointless now, but you can see how important time (timing) is to the outcome of many situations.

I know I have arrived at a good place in my life and I know that might not be so, if I had done anything differently, but I look back now at so many seemingly wasted opportunities and I'd like to be given the chance to revisit them and make those minutes and hours so much more meaningful. Many of the significant moments in our lives only come around once and any given second might be a momentous opportunity. Benjamin Franklin once said: *"Dost thou love life? Then do not squander time, for it is the stuff life is made of."*

It is physically impossible (at least as far as we know) to turn back the hands of time. They only move forward; but I know each moment of my life that passes puts me that much closer to being with Ethan and everyone else I love, who has passed from this life; this world of time. In eternity there is no time as we know it and missed opportunities come back around repeatedly, as if on a wheel, endlessly in motion.

53

I WALK THE LINE

The Bible tells us we are to live "in the world", but not be "of the world". What does this mean? I was always puzzled about those words; if we were sent here from heaven to live, how could we not be "of the world?" This question has been answered for me because of my "spiritually transformative experience". Since the day I looked into the eyes of Jesus, as I sat next to Ethan's casket,
He has become a companion; as it says in the old hymn "In the Garden", he walks with me and he talks with me. What that means is that I now have an awareness that He is close to me in spirit, so I know that even in the worst times, I am never alone; I don't have to face anything alone and I never did. How I wish I had known that for the first 64 years of my life.

Having an STE doesn't mean I live life like a nun in the cloister; I don't spend every minute of every day in prayer. It doesn't mean I can't have a conversation with someone that doesn't include beating them over the head with my Bible. What it does mean is that my life has become fully entwined with Jesus' teachings, and that has opened up all of the spiritual gifts He wants me to have. It has opened up a world of knowledge that doesn't come from my own thinking mind.

I know I'm not making up all of these things and I know they are more real than anything I can see with my earthly eyes; knowing this gives me the courage to write and speak about these things with a boldness that is not my own.

Before I experienced this transformation, I would have been very hesitant to say or write many of the things I feel compelled to share with others; especially in such a public way. I have no formal training of any kind; I'm not a Bible scholar, I have no formal religious training or college experience of any kind to support the things I say. I'm not trained as a public speaker. Amazingly, in spite of my feelings of ineptitude, not one single person has questioned my right to say what I know is true, or the validity of what I say or write. If they had, I would hope I would handle the challenge to my beliefs with kindness and grace. It wouldn't change anything I know is true, if such a challenge were issued, because I speak from my own experiences; no one told me to say these things; they are true to me because I have lived them. I can't prove to anyone that what I say is true, is so; nor can I prove I have had any of the experiences I relate; still, that doesn't invalidate any of it. It is always my fervent prayer that I not say anything that would cause someone to disbelieve or to turn away from God; you can call Him whatever name suits you, I knew Him for most of my life as God. I am comfortable now calling Him by many names; but it doesn't matter, because as I recently saw somewhere in one of the numerous books I read: God knows who He is; it really doesn't matter what you call him, as long as you make the effort to know Him.

When I began to read voraciously, following Ethan's passing, I realized I was not alone in my seeking or in what I was experiencing. Many others have written very similar accounts; having said that, let me say in all truthfulness: I had never even heard of those books, nor read one until after my spiritual experiences began to happen. My point is this: Don't assume because I have read them now, that I merely gleaned my information from reading the accounts written by others. Every single experience written about in this book is my own; period!

In all the years prior to Ethan's passing, I lived a very small percentage of my life spiritually; I would estimate it to be only about 10% of my time that was focused on God or spiritual thinking. I'm sure this is pretty common in today's world. Now, I would estimate that about 80% of my time is focused on spirit. There is a distinct point at which most people shift from human awareness or being, to spiritual awareness; this is the "line" this chapter is referring to. As you begin to increase the time you spend in spiritual thinking or "being", the line begins to blur and you find yourself more easily moving from one side of the line to the other. With the spiritual growth that resulted from my experience of deep grief, I am able to make that shift hundreds of times each day.

We are not meant to be only spiritual while living as human beings; that is what we do when we return to the world of spirit (what some call heaven, nirvana, paradise etc.) at that point we are spiritual beings with human experience. Our human experiences are meant to help us grow spiritually. If we believe we are only human beings and that what happens in this world is the "main event", we return to the world of spirit having gained very little of real significance.

In my search for answers, I have come to believe, as many do, that the Earth is merely a place to learn specific things; before I began my search in earnest, I couldn't have told you what I was sent here to learn, and now I know the most important of these things was forgiveness.

I was unable to learn to forgive, until I found myself having to contemplate forgiving the unthinkable, the murder of my son. I had a very clear choice before me; it was starkly black and white with absolutely no gray area or blurred lines. The choice came down to this: forgive this man or hold onto anger and bitterness and make my life a living hell; a death of my humanity.

I don't want to give anyone the impression that as soon as I forgave the man who took Ethan's life, everything became sunshine and roses; there were still oceans of tears and seemingly endless days of pain and despair; my heart was still broken and no amount of time will make it as good as new.

What forgiveness did was open the door to a new life; a life very much like the one that died when Ethan passed, but a life where pain isn't in control of all I do. Forgiveness wasn't excusing what happened; it was merely accepting that it happened. I will never be "okay" with it and I'm not required to; but since the moment I forgave Shannon for his actions that caused me the worst pain I have ever had to endure, forgiveness of anything else that happens is easy. What I have received from God in return for that forgiveness is indescribably precious, and knowing I was able to learn the most important lesson of my life, fills me with a great sense of accomplishment and deep peace.

54

I SURRENDER ALL

I believe there is a tremendous misunderstanding regarding what it means to surrender in a spiritual sense. As with so many things, modern western religions manage to make it seem like a negative thing; many people view it as having to give up something. They see it as a loss or a sacrifice, and that isn't an idea that appeals to a lot of people. I see it in the way many others who don't ascribe to traditional religious views do; it simply means that you get yourself (ego) out of the way and give spirit room to work. It has nothing to do with surrendering your free will; that is yours to keep.
I used to feel the way most people feel about it, especially those raised in traditional congregations in this country. I felt that way because I was taught to believe that way and it is incredibly hard to abandon those things we were taught to believe as children.

At the point my belief changed, after my son's passing, I realized I wasn't so much giving up something as I was acknowledging my helplessness and inability to go any further without divine assistance. I couldn't see a way to go forward; not even to take the first step toward healing. I thought my life was over, even though I was still physically alive. When you can't just die and you can't move forward, something else has to happen. In my case, it was God; the only thing that hadn't been shaken by the murder of my son. My belief in the love of God was all I had to hold onto. I will never stop being grateful beyond imagination that God was there when I reached out to Him.

Without the limitations or road blocks I had built up in my relationship with God, who is the source of all that exists, all that has ever existed, and all that will come into being in the future, He was free to give me a continuous flow of love and support. These gifts of love and compassion began to rain down on me consistently and it is hard to remember a time when I didn't receive them. Perhaps, they have always been there, but I was just unable to see them for what they were. When Ethan's life was taken, I couldn't believe it was possible for me to live any kind of meaningful life going forward. I had no idea I would be living a life as blessed as the one God has provided for me.

If you look at the definitions of the word surrender, you will find they all sound negative. In our society surrendering means you are the loser; in a spiritual sense it means opening the door to the greatest gift; a win like no other. What you gain in the act of fully recognizing God's majesty, is simply everything. You are showered with unconditional love and support. You are given knowledge you never believed it was possible for human beings to possess. Hopelessness and doubt disappear and you know you have never been alone, nor could you ever be. In the moment you fully acknowledge God and put your trust in Him completely, something mystical takes place.

That doesn't mean you will never again suffer grief or the sadness of loss. It doesn't mean you will never suffer disappointment or struggle; it means you will never struggle alone and you will always be given exactly what you need to get through it. There will always be guidance and meaning in the struggle. You will be able to see the path that leads you out of the darkness and even in times of trial you will have peace in your spirit and an abiding love in your heart. You will see just how deeply you are loved and you will be humbled by the love and compassion of the Divine Presence.

When I thought about compiling my spiritual experiences into one book, it was about showing the totality of them (so far, at least) to illustrate that these things become an everyday occurrence. I am changed; my life is changed. Through the terrible loss of my son, God made something meaningful and beautiful and while it doesn't change the fact that Ethan isn't here with us; it makes missing him so much more bearable for me. I feel his presence with me every day in so many little ways and nothing could give me more comfort than that. Having these experiences is like finding buried treasure time after time; they bring joy and light into my life, and I will never cease to be humbled by them.

55

I HOPE YOU DANCE

Many of the things I've written about are a reflection of what I see when I peer into the pool of water that is my past. In a previous book, I stated that I'm looking at my past in order to find the future. As I look back, I am surprised to find so much more there than I would have expected to discover.

I'm not just looking for memories, though that is what one usually expects to find in the past. I am looking for my soul, my spirit, my true and eternal self. I am also surprised to find that this is a journey of love; self-love. As a person who lived with an inferiority complex for many years, that comes as a shock. I lived through a period of time in the past when I became lost to myself; I didn't know or recognize the person I had become and I didn't like her and certainly didn't love her.

It is a humbling experience to find in myself, someone I have come to love. I don't love myself in a proud or egotistical way; I love the self in me that God loves and I forgive her for all of the mistakes she has made and I apologize to her for all of the times I judged her so harshly. She has walked through the fires of loss and she has been wounded by the experience, but at the same time she has been healed by it. She has learned to recognize Truth and she has gained wisdom and she is at peace with herself. She has found wonder and meaning in the small things that so often went unnoticed in her past, and she will not let herself overlook them in the future. She has learned to embrace her joy and her pain as part of the same heart; without them life would have no meaning. She has learned to sing from her soul and to dance in the rain. She has learned to do all that she does with gratitude and compassion. I am so eager to learn what else is waiting to be discovered in the depths of my soul.

As for you, I hope you will find peace as well, and" I hope you dance", which is just another way of saying; I hope you will learn to live every precious moment of your life in a meaningful way and in joyous celebration.

56

FEELS SO RIGHT

When I wrote my first book, I thought that I would dot the last I and cross the last T, and then I would put it away and not go back to that story again. I envisioned my family pulling it out of my cedar chest one day in the future, after I had passed. I pictured them reliving our great tragedy through my eyes and my perspective.

Instead, I was led in a spiritual sense to self-publish it and share it with others; that was initially a scary thought for me. The first people to read it were members of my own family; that wasn't so hard. Then I shared it with some of my closest friends and that wasn't so bad either, but it wasn't enough. I knew I was supposed to use it to try to help other people that I didn't even know and who had no prior knowledge of me, my character or credibility. I thought surely they would assume I was unstable, or a scam artist or just a liar. In spite of that possibility, I knew I was supposed to share my story, no matter what reaction I got.

When I began to speak publicly about the loss of my son and my personal transformation, I found it impacted me emotionally, in ways I never imagined. It gave me strength, and from somewhere outside myself came courage, that wasn't my own. Then I began to hear myself saying things I had never intended to say; words that also came from outside myself. Putting it that way sounds crazy even to me, but I know it isn't crazy at all. It's more normal than the majority of experiences that make up my life. It feels so right; all the way to the depths of my soul. That's the reason I haven't been able to stop writing.

I have often described the transition I am going through as a journey. That feels right too, because it has been a progression; it began the moment I heard that Ethan was no longer living in this world, and it continues still. It has taken me to places I didn't intend to go and to places I didn't imagine it was possible to go. It has taken me light years away from familiar beliefs and people. These are people I am so grateful to have shared a portion of my life with, but I am no longer able to communicate with them because I have moved spiritually, to a place they are unable to relate to and we no longer share common ground or even the same language. They are speaking midwestern and I am speaking lightworker. They don't understand what's happened. Why am I not the person they have known for decades?

It is all perfectly clear to me, but it's as if they all have amnesia. My guidance is telling me I must move on from people, places and things that no longer serve my spiritual growth, but I struggle with the appearance that I am abandoning people who have treated me well and supported me through many of my life's losses. I don't want anyone to feel mistreated or abandoned by me; they have done nothing wrong. It is me who has changed so drastically and it is another piece of fallout from the explosion that rocked my world when Ethan was murdered.

I knew this would happen; I knew it had to happen, but I mourn these losses as well. I hope those who feel wounded by it will forgive me in time; I hope they will come to see the enormity of the call I feel to do something more meaningful; something I couldn't do as that person they used to know. I can only leave them with my fondest wishes that they be showered with blessings in the lives they are leading, and my love and gratitude for eternity.

57

CRYSTAL BLUE PERSUASION

*O*ne of the things that bothers me most about the world of time, as I see it through the lens of personal spiritual growth, is the fact that we have been so indoctrinated into the thinking of this world, that we choose to believe a story that makes absolutely no sense, and which causes many of us to live out our time here in confusion and pain. It isn't easy to break free from the world's fractured fairytale; as human beings we are taught to reject anything that doesn't fit the accepted belief system. Most often, something tragic or at the very least dramatic has to occur in our lives in order for us to be blasted out of our allegiance to the false narrative the world teaches. In my case, it took the death of my son to shatter the illusion.

It wasn't that I never questioned the world's version of things, but since we are programmed to believe that if something doesn't make sense or add up the way you believe it should, you just tell yourself: *"I'll understand it when I get to the next world"*, or *"There are some things that won't be revealed to us until we cross over to the other side."* I was willing to accept that answer for most of my life.

I have had hundreds of experiences and revelations since

Ethan's passing that show me how misguided our thinking is about life and death. Many of those things, I believed could not be known before passing from this world, I now have the answer to and those answers make perfect sense, in ways the accepted paradigm never did.

One of the misperceptions the world fosters is that it isn't possible to communicate with our loved ones who have passed from human existence and that it is sinful to try to do so. That misguided belief causes such overwhelming grief and sadness for millions of people on this planet. I know this concept is false; I know it from the things I have experienced since Ethan's passing. No one has indoctrinated me into believing a lie or brainwashed me in some way; these are my own experiences that actually began years prior to the act that took Ethan's physical life.

The religious teachings of churches in the western world rob those in deep grief of comfort and peace, all the while believing that what they offer is what is appropriate and all that is needed. I once presented the first book I wrote to the pastor of the Protestant church I was attending; he thanked me and has rarely spoken to me since; that is how I know he read it.

Don't misunderstand me; I believe the message of acceptance, forgiveness, love, hope and peace that Jesus came into the world to deliver, but I believe that message has been turned into something other than what it was intended to be. It is no longer a message of acceptance and forgiveness, but a condemnation of those Jesus came to help. *"God is love.",* the Bible says so, but God is presented as a wrathful, judgmental deity. The message of love and forgiveness is rarely mentioned; the Holy Spirit has become only a concept and not an active force for teaching and revelation. In John 4:24 KJV, Jesus says: *"God is a spirit and they that worship Him, must worship Him in spirit and in truth."* In Luke 17:20, Jesus said: *"The kingdom of God is within you."* My experiences have shown me that it is indeed, inside each of us. That is not to be taken to mean that it is not real; it is more real than that which we see around us now.

I find that today's churches are uncomfortable with talk of spirits; it doesn't fit their paradigm. They believe anyone who claims to have contact with deceased spirits is a liar or a charlatan and most of all, a sinner. Think of all the things Jesus did and then remember that He said it is possible for us to do these things and things even greater than He did.

Those who are able to tap into the ability to see and perceive these things, bring real comfort to those who suffer nearly unbearable pain. This pain comes from the separation with their loved ones, that our accepted beliefs regarding death bring about. Many people believe God wants us to suffer and that unless we do, we are not worthy of His love. God loves us unconditionally and it makes no sense that He would want us to suffer, or be the cause of such pain.

I asked for God's help and what came to me was almost immediate and continuing contact with my deceased son. I didn't initiate the first contacts with him and since that day, my prayer has been to speak only the Truth that has been revealed to me and to never mislead anyone as to what has happened in my life, since these experiences began. If I have deliberately sinned or out of ignorance, misinterpreted what happens to me, why am I blessed beyond imagination, as I tell my story to others?

Human beings often confer upon God, human like behavior; human beings as a whole are very negative in their thinking; our programming in negativity begins almost as soon as we emerge from the womb and take our first breath. Finding our way back to the world we came from isn't easy, but it's much simpler than we are led to believe.

> In God's amazing love,
> J.S

FINAL WORD

I am always so grateful and honored when someone reads my books. I hope this book has given you something of value; something positive. I hope it has given you food for thought. I hope you will share it with someone you know.

I wish for us all a more peaceful and harmonious world. Only Love can create that and we can support it by letting our own light of love and peace shine brightly and join with others who do the same.

I thank you!
J. S. Schmidt

ACKNOWLEDGEMENTS

ONE:……………………………….R.Gibb,B.Gibb,M.Gibb
TWO FACES HAVE I.………………......….L.Christie,T.Herbert
SONG FOR ALL LOVERS.…………………………..J.Denver
HOOKED ON A FEELING.……………......……….. M.James
DOES ANYBODY REALLY KNOW WHAT TIME IT IS?...R. Lamm
POWER IN THE BLOOD.………….....…………...L.E. Jones
OPEN MY EYES THAT I MAY SEE..…....……......…..C.H. Scott
HEAVENLY SUNLIGHT.………….....…………….G.H. Cook
INTO THE MYSTIC.……………..........…….…….Van Morrison
LADY.……………………….......………….…..L.Richey
WEDDING BELL BLUES.…………......………….….L. Nyro
I'VE GOT YOU UNDER MY SKIN.………...……….….C.Porter
GYPSY WOMAN.……………..…………….B.McDill, A.Reynolds
THE HOUSE YOU LIVE IN.……….......……………G.Lightfoot
I SAW THE LIGHT.……………….....……………H.Williams
WINGS OF A DOVE.…………….....………….…...B.Ferguson
PRECIOUS ANGEL/SHINE YOUR LIGHT...…………….B.Dylan
RUN FOR THE ROSES.………………......………….D.Fogelberg
FIRE AND RAIN.…………………………........…….J. Taylor
VISIONS OF JOHANNA.……………….…………….B.Dylan
ONCE IN A RED MOON.……………………...…….R.Loveland
STRANGE.…………………….........……….M.Tillis,F.Burch

SNAPSHOT.................................D. Morgan, R. Fleming
SMOKE GETS IN YOUR EYES..................O. Harbach, J. Kern
SMOKE ON THE WATER.......................R. Glover, I. Gillian
WILDWOOD FLOWER..........................A.P. Carter
LAY DOWN BESIDE ME.......................D. Williams
A LIVING PRAYER..........................R. Block
COAT OF MANY COLORS......................D. Parton
JUST AS I AM.............................C. Elliot
THE EAGLE AND THE HAWK...................J. Denver
DEEP IN THE HEART OF TEXAS...............J. Hershey, D. Swander
ANGEL EYES...............................M. Dennis, E. Brent
MAMA.....................................M. James
ALL THAT HEAVEN WILL ALLOW...............B. Springsteen
WHERE HAVE YOU GONE?.....................M. Reynolds
I SURRENDER ALL..........................J. Van Deventer
PACHELBEL'S CANON IN D...................J. Pachelbel
BUTTERFLY KISSES.........................B. Carlisle, R. Thomas
ISLE OF ST. HELENA.......................Unknown source
FUNNY HOW TIME SLIPS AWAY................Willie Nelson
I WALK THE LINE..........................J. Cash
I HOPE YOU DANCE.........................M. Sanders, T. Sillers
DIAMOND GIRL.............................J. Seals, D. Crofts
GLORY DAYS...............................B. Springsteen
TRACES OF LOVE...........................Cobb, Gordy, Bruie
FLY AWAY.................................J. Denver
IN THE GARDEN............................C. Miles, R. Hebble
THE MESSENGER............................R. Blackmore
UNDER HIS WINGS..........................W. Cushing
BROWN EYED GIRL..........................V. Morrison

EVERYTHING I OWN..D.Gates
SCHEHERAZADE..R.Korsakov
FLIGHT OF THE BUMBLEBEE.......................... R.Korsakov
LAYLA...E.Clapton
THE VILLAGE LANTERNE...................C.Night,R.Blackmore
PEACE,PEACE/SILENT NIGHT.......F.Gruber,J.F.Young,J.Mohr
WALK THROUGH THIS WORLD WITH ME...Seamons,Savage
I AM YOUR ANGEL..R.Kelly
UNDER THE DOUBLE EAGLE..................................J.F. Wagner
LONGER..D. Fogelberg
EVERYTHING I OWN...D. Gates
BROWN EYED GIRL...V. Morrison

www.ingramcontent.com/pod-product-compliance
Lightning Source LLC
Chambersburg PA
CBHW060405160426
42811CB00089B/2374/J